INTRODUCTION TO
PROBLEM SOLVING

INTRODUCTION TO PROBLEM SOLVING

Strategies for the Elementary Math Classroom

Susan O'Connell

HEINEMANN
Portsmouth, NH

Heinemann
A division of Reed Elsevier Inc.
361 Hanover Street
Portsmouth, NH 03801–3912
www.heinemann.com

Offices and agents throughout the world

The author and publisher wish to thank those who have generously given permission to reprint borrowed material:

"1–100 Chart" adapted from Marilyn Burns (1992). *About Teaching Mathematics*, page 131. Copyright © 1992 by Math Solutions Publications. All rights reserved. Reprinted by permission.

A special thanks to the following problem solvers, whose work samples appear in this book: Kari Adlington, Catherine Blackwood, Jared Brown, Keegan Girouard, Emily Hall, Aaron Harten, Ben Hazel, Julie Hetrick, Aaron Lair, Rachel Lair, Jessica Lietz, Lindsay Littlejohn, Emil Mentz, Haley Nalley, Steven O'Connell, Toyin Orunja, Susan Pinson, and Justin Sosebee.

Library of Congress Cataloging-in-Publication Data
O'Connell, Sue.
    Introduction to problem solving : strategies for the elementary math classroom / Sue O'Connell.
        p.   cm.
    Includes bibliographical references.
    ISBN 0-325-00199-5
    1. Problem solving—Study and teaching (Elementary).   I. Title.
    QA63.O36   2000
    370.15′24—dc21   99-055425

Editor: Susan Ohanian
Production coordinator: Elizabeth Valway
Production: Matrix Productions
Cover design: Joni Doherty Design
Manufacturing: Deanna Richardson

Printed in the United States of America on acid-free paper
10 09 08 07 06 VP 9 10 11 12 13

To Brendan and Katie,
for the time we spent solving math problems together

Contents

ONE   AN INTRODUCTION TO PROBLEM-SOLVING
INSTRUCTION   1

Why Teach Problem Solving?   1

Creating Effective Problem Solvers   1

Developing Skills and Attitudes   2

How This Book Will Help You   3

TWO   GUIDING STUDENTS THROUGH THE PROBLEM-
SOLVING PROCESS   5

Breaking Down the Process   5

    Step 1: Understand the Question   5

    Step 2: Choose a Plan   6

    Step 3: Try Your Plan   6

    Step 4: Check Your Answer   7

    Step 5: Reflect on What You've Done   7

Using a Checklist with Students   8

Helping Students Get "Unstuck"   8

Involving Students in Instruction   8

CONTENTS

THREE   ASSESSING PROBLEM SOLVING   11

The Role of Ongoing Assessment   11

The Value of Observations   12

The Value of Rubrics in Assessment   12

A Holistic Rubric for Problem Solving   13

The Role of Rubrics in Improvement   15

Analytic Rubrics for Assessing Specific Skills   15

    Outcome 1: Select and Use an Appropriate Strategy   16

    Outcome 2: Calculate a Correct Answer   16

    Outcome 3: Communicate Mathematically   16

Self-Reflections on Problem Solving   18

Varied Assessment   18

FOUR   STRATEGY: CHOOSE AN OPERATION   19

Key Words Versus Key Concepts   19

Practice with Recognizing Key Concepts   20

    Addition   20

    Subtraction   20

    Multiplication   20

    Division   20

Practice with Choosing the Correct Operation   21

    Group Activities and Discussions   21

    Pinch Cards   21

    Student-Created Problems   22

A Look at Student Work   23

Reflecting on the Strategy   23

Selecting Practice Problems   23

FIVE   STRATEGY: FIND A PATTERN   25

Discovering a Variety of Patterns   25

Completing and Describing Number Patterns   26

Working with Geometric Patterns   27

| | A Look at Student Work | 28 |
| | Reflecting on the Strategy | 28 |

SIX	STRATEGY: MAKE A TABLE	31
	Constructing a Table	31
	Recognizing and Extending Patterns	32
	Deciding When to Stop the Pattern	32
	Selecting the Correct Answer	32
	Solving More Sophisticated Table Problems	33
	A Look at Student Work	34
	Reflecting on the Strategy	35

SEVEN	STRATEGY: MAKE AN ORGANIZED LIST	37
	Organization Is the Key	37
	Working from Concrete to Abstract	38
	Laying the Foundation for More Sophisticated Skills	38
	A Look at Student Work	39
	Reflecting on the Strategy	40

EIGHT	STRATEGY: DRAW A PICTURE OR DIAGRAM	41
	A New Meaning for the Word *Picture*	42
	A Look at Student Work	43
	Reflecting on the Strategy	44

NINE	STRATEGY: GUESS, CHECK, AND REVISE	45
	Beginning with a Guess	45
	Revising the Guess	45
	Using Guess, Check, and Revise with Equations	46
	Understanding the Role of Positive Attitudes	46
	A Look at Student Work	46
	Building the Foundation for More Advanced Skills	48
	Reflecting on the Strategy	48

TEN	STRATEGY: USE LOGICAL REASONING	49
	Using a Logic Matrix	50
	Using a List of Organize Clues	50
	Using a Venn Diagram to Organize Ideas	51
	A Look at Student Work	51
	Reflecting on the Strategy	52
ELEVEN	STRATEGY: WORK BACKWARD	53
	Working Backward with Equations	54
	A Look at Student Work	54
	Reflecting on the Strategy	56
TWELVE	REAL-WORLD PROBLEM SOLVING	57
	Creating Meaningful Real-World Tasks	57
	Applying Classroom Skills to Meaningful Tasks	58
	Utilizing the Messiness of Real-World Data	59
	Discovering a World of Real Data	60
	Newspapers	60
	Restaurant Menus	61
	Recipes	61
	Travel Brochures	61
	Catalogs	61
	Grocery Ads	62
	Sports Schedules	62
	Sports Player Cards	62
	Nutritional Labels	63
	Advertisements	63
	Reaping the Benefit of Real-World Activities	63
THIRTEEN	ACCEPTING THE CHALLENGE	65
	The Challenge to Educators	65
APPENDIXES		
	A Problem-Solving Checklists	67
	B Key Concepts Posters	71

C   Observation Checklist   77

D   Assessment Tools   81

E   Pinch Cards   87

F   Strategy Icons   91

G   Practice Problems   95

H   Real-World Problem-Solving Resources   173

I   Parent Letter: Tips for Helping Your Child Get "Unstuck"   187

REFERENCES   189

INTRODUCTION TO
PROBLEM SOLVING

CHAPTER ONE

An Introduction to Problem-Solving Instruction

Problem solving should be the central focus of the mathematics

curriculum. As such, it is a primary goal of all mathematics

instruction and an integral part of all mathematical activity. Problem

solving is not a distinct topic but a process that should permeate the

entire program and provide the context in which concepts and skills

can be learned.   NCTM

Why Teach Problem Solving?

Traditionally, problem solving has been viewed as a distinct topic, introduced to students after they've mastered basic skills. In recent mathematics reform, triggered by the National Council of Teachers of Mathematics' *Curriculum and Evaluation Standards for School Mathematics*, problem solving is considered a critical part of mathematics instruction. Problem solving is the reason we teach mathematics. Our goal is to enable students to use their mathematical knowledge to solve problems. With the advent of the NCTM Standards, problem solving has been recognized as central to an effective instructional program. Teachers begin skills lessons by posing a problem, then they teach a skill to help solve the problem, and the newly acquired skill allows students to successfully find a

solution. Problem solving becomes both the starting point and the ending point to well-balanced mathematics lessons. Developing students' computational skills is important, and teaching those skills in a problem-solving context ensures that students not only understand the skill but see the meaningfulness of learning the skill and understand how to apply it to real-world situations. "Problem solving is the process by which students experience the power and usefulness of mathematics in the world around them" (NCTM 1989, 75).

Creating Effective Problem Solvers

My teaching experiences have convinced me that problem solving must be systematically taught to students. In my early experiences with teaching problem solving, I began much like my own teachers had, assigning problems to students and expecting them to be able to solve the problems on their own. I quickly recognized my students' anxiety and frustration. I soon learned that assigning problems and then correcting those problems did not create successful problem solvers. I began to break down the skills needed to solve problems and teach my students specific strategies to help them organize their thinking. The more strategies that I was able to share with my students, the more successful they became. Surprisingly, not just the most capable of my students showed progress, but all of them did. As I demonstrated various strategies to attack problems and began to let my students *see* math problems through visual and hands-on demonstrations, their skills improved. And my skills improved, too! The more comfortable I became at teaching problem solving, the more confident I became about my ability to help students understand a process that had once seemed so complicated and abstract.

With an understanding of the problem-solving process and a repertoire of strategies to assist students in dealing with problem situations, your anxiety and frustration will lessen and your enthusiasm and confidence will grow. Not all students can become effective problem solvers on their own, but with the help of a confident and capable teacher, all students can develop into effective problem solvers.

Developing Skills and Attitudes

Developing students' problem-solving abilities is a challenging and complex task. It requires attention to the building of mathematical skills and thinking processes as well as attention to the development of positive attitudes toward problem solving. Both skills and attitudes must be strengthened to produce truly effective problem solvers.

Problem solving is a process, requiring students to follow a series of steps to find a solution. Although some students may intuitively follow a process, most students need to

be taught how to proceed through steps to reach a solution. Another important goal in teaching students to solve problems is assisting them in developing strategies or plans for solving problems. While choosing a mathematical operation—addition, subtraction, multiplication, or division—is frequently the way to solve a problem, alternate strategies are often needed. Helping students learn strategies such as drawing pictures, finding patterns, making tables, making lists, guessing and checking, working backward, or using logical reasoning gives students a wide variety of strategies to employ during problem solving. Problem solving requires this knowledge of strategies as well as the ability to determine when each strategy would be best used. The more students practice these strategies, the more confident they become in their ability to solve problems and apply mathematics in meaningful ways.

The development of a positive attitude toward problem solving is crucial to student success. Teachers are instrumental in helping students develop the attitudes needed to become successful problem solvers.

Problem solving requires patience. It is not always possible to find a quick answer and quick answers are often incorrect. Problem solving is not judged on speed but on the reasonableness of the final solution.

Problem solving requires persistence. Students may need to try several strategies before finding one that will work. Students must have confidence that they can find a solution, even if it is not immediately apparent.

Problem solving requires risk taking. Students need to be willing to try their "hunches," hoping that they may lead to a solution. Students must feel comfortable making mistakes, as problem solving is a process filled with mistakes that often lead to the solution.

Problem solving requires cooperation. Students must often be willing to share ideas, build on one another's thoughts, and work together to find a solution.

Students become successful problem solvers when they are instructed in a climate that rewards patience, persistence, risk taking, and cooperation. The teacher has a critical role in establishing a positive climate for problem-solving instruction.

How This Book Will Help You

This book is designed to help you better understand problem-solving instruction. It includes information on helping students understand the problem-solving process as well as information on teaching specific strategies including Choose an Operation; Find a Pattern; Make a Table; Make an Organized List; Draw a Picture or Diagram; Guess, Check, and Revise; Use Logical Reasoning; and Work Backward. I share ideas for introducing each strategy to students in a visual or hands-on way. These introductory lessons are not grade level specific but rather depend on the students' prior knowledge or their previous exposure to the strategy. In all cases, students at the second-grade level can be exposed to the introductory lesson, but a similar activity may be appropriate for older students who have never been exposed to the strategy. Although second-grade work samples are the earliest samples provided in this book, students can begin to develop many of the strategies including finding patterns, making lists and tables, and drawing pictures in kindergarten or first grade. At these levels, visual and hands-on examples are essential to instruction.

For each strategy, I share teacher tips that highlight some important points to emphasize when working with students. Examples of student work are presented for each strategy, including samples of students' communications about their problem solving. The work samples will help you see the progression of skills, and the writing samples offer a glimpse into students' thinking as their problem-solving skills develop. The final chapter will provide you with ideas for connecting problem solving to your students' lives. Ideas for using real-world data and materials are presented.

The appendixes contain a variety of materials to help you implement a problem-solving program in your classroom. Checklists, evaluation forms, scoring keys, and icons are all available as well as a variety of practice problems for your students. The activities range from simple to complex. Select those activities that suit your students' level of expertise, and continue to challenge your students with more sophisticated thinking as their skills improve.

This book was developed as a result of my extensive reading of problem-solving theory, my reflection on current practices, and my observations on the progress of students in a classroom setting. As a result of both research and practice, I have adapted and modified some common problem-solving techniques, developed some new activities to support problem-solving instruction, and highlighted resources and activities that are particularly effective for the elementary grades. It is hoped that this book will encourage you to reflect on the teaching of mathematical problem solving as you evaluate your current teaching techniques and expand your teaching repertoire with new strategies and ideas. Most certainly, as your teaching skills increase, your students' problem-solving skills will increase as well.

CHAPTER TWO

Guiding Students Through the Problem-Solving Process

Through group and classroom discussions, students can examine a

variety of approaches and learn to evaluate appropriate strategies for a

given solution. The instructional goal is that students will build an

increasing repertoire of strategies, approaches, and familiar problems;

it is the problem-solving process that is most important, not just the

answer. NCTM

Problem solving is a multistep task. Successful problem solvers systematically proceed through a series of steps toward the solution. Helping students see this progression will help them view problem solving as a process in which they organize their actions in a logical and sequential way. The more proficient a student becomes, the more quickly he or she will move through these steps; but initially, focusing students on each step will ensure that they have considered the data, developed a logical plan of action, and carried out the plan in an accurate and reasonable way. Following is a checklist that guides students through the critical steps of the problem-solving process:

Problem-Solving Checklist
Understand the question.
Choose a plan.
Try your plan.
Check your answer.
Reflect on what you've done.

Breaking Down the Process

Step 1: Understand the Question
This first step in the problem-solving process asks students to think about the problem and decide *what* they are being asked to solve. This is an important step in focusing students for the problem-solving process ahead. If students are uncertain what they are being asked to solve, the likelihood that they will successfully progress through the remaining steps is poor. In this step, students restate the problem in their own words, explaining what it is asking them to do. Students might be given written problems and asked to identify the question, either by circling the "question"

part of the problem or by writing the question in their own words. You might direct them to work in pairs or groups to determine what the problem is asking them to do. Hearing one another's thoughts will strengthen their skills for understanding problems. You could also ask students to select and circle the data that they believe will be needed to solve the problem, and discussions might focus on the types of data that will be helpful to them. When practicing this step, students do not need to solve each problem that is posed to them. When students isolate the skill of identifying and understanding the question and practice that skill without moving through all of the steps of the problem-solving process, they strengthen their skills in this area.

Step 2: Choose a Plan

In this critical step, students must decide *how* to solve the problem. Students will need to identify a plan or *strategy* for solving the problem. Students may recognize that the problem can be solved with one of the basic operations—addition, subtraction, multiplication, or division—or they may discover that an alternate strategy—making a list, table, or diagram; working backward; finding a pattern; guessing, checking, and revising; or using logical reasoning—may be more effective for

solving the problem. Students may look for key concepts to help them decide on a strategy or may relate the problem to other familiar problems in order to help them decide how to proceed. Often, more than one strategy can be used to solve a problem. Discussions at this stage will help students appreciate the different ways that problems can be solved. The more practice that students have in deciding on an appropriate strategy, the more skilled they will become at selecting a strategy on their own.

Step 3: Try Your Plan

Now it's time to put the selected strategy to use. In this step, the student will use his or her strategy to attempt to find a solution. Encourage the use of calculators during this step. Using calculators helps students focus on the problem-solving process. Often, students' anxiety or confusion regarding the calculations distracts them from the primary objective of the lesson, which relates to their problem-solving skills. If you are assessing students' ability to solve problems, calculators will help both you and the students focus on the problem-solving objectives. The use of calculators also reduces the amount of time needed to calculate answers and so gives students more time to spend on the "thinking" part of

---

CLASSROOM-TESTED TIP

Estimating the Answer

Once students have decided on their plan for solving a problem, it is a good time for them to stop and think about what the predicted answer will be. When students are able to predict or estimate the answer, they are better able to judge the reasonableness of the answer when they calculate it later in the process. Many errors occur when students make calculation mistakes and have not previously considered what the answer might be. Without a predicted answer, an inappropriate calculation may not be noticed. Seeing a discrepancy between his or her predicted answer and a cal-

culated answer sends up a red flag, alerting the student to take a second look at the answer.

There may be times when predicting an answer is difficult. It is easy to do some quick mental math to estimate that 5 and 13 will be about 20. But some problems, for example those for which a diagram might be needed to find a solution, will be difficult for students to predict. Predicting is a step that can help students later in the process. If they are unable to do it, it's okay; teach students to move on and continue with the remaining steps in the problem-solving process.

the process. Most importantly, it helps students recognize the significant and appropriate role of technology in assisting them in finding solutions.

At times, students may try their plans and find that they do not lead to a solution. This is an important realization. Students need to recognize that trying and then eliminating a strategy is okay. Finding a solution does not always happen on the first try. Recognizing that a strategy was unsuccessful and deciding on another strategy are important skills in building effective problem solvers.

Step 4: Check Your Answer

Traditionally, this step has focused on checking for calculation errors. While checking for arithmetic accuracy is important, it is equally important that students recognize that checking their answers includes checking the reasonableness of the answers. If students were able to predict an answer before trying their plans, this is the time for them to compare their predicted and actual answers to see if they are compatible. Encourage students to ask themselves questions like "Does this answer make sense? Does something seem not quite right?"

Even without a prediction, students are often able to recognize when an answer does not seem reasonable. Asking students to write a summary sentence that relates their answer

to the question will force them to look at the question and their answer together and will often help them detect unreasonable answers. This technique is especially helpful for those students who rush from problem to problem, doing the calculations and never looking back to check for reasonableness.

Consider the following problem:

There were 500 students at the assembly. 240 students were boys. How many girls were at the assembly?

Summary sentence: There were 500 students at the assembly; 240 of them were boys, and 740 of them were girls.

The realization: *"That can't be right! There were only 500 students there."*

Step 5: Reflect on What You've Done

Once the problem has been solved, it is time for students to sit back and reflect on what they did throughout the process. You might ask students to explain how they solved the problem or to justify their solution. You might ask them to share other ways of solving the problem or reflect on what was easy or hard about the task. This step allows students to process what they've done, and it gives teachers valuable insight into students' thinking.

CLASSROOM-TESTED TIP

Modeling Your Thinking

The think-aloud is a very valuable tool in teaching problem solving. During a think-aloud, the teacher says aloud what she is thinking while working through the problem. Students are able to hear the teacher's thoughts as she analyzes the situation and makes decisions:

"Let's see—I know that every basket has the same number of apples in it. That tells me I can use multiplication. I'll just look

back at the question to check how many apples are in each basket."

or

"I predicted that the answer would be 12, but I got 130. Something is not right. It wouldn't make sense for the answer to be 130. I think I'll go back and check my calculations to see if I made a mistake."

Teachers who are cognizant of common errors can direct their think-alouds to those mistakes.

Using a Checklist with Students

As with many skills that are multistep, showing students how to monitor the problem-solving process through the use of a checklist will help them work in an organized, step-by-step fashion. Initially, students will need to be taught what is required at each step of the process. They will need to see the steps modeled and they will need to move slowly through each step until it becomes routine. In the early stages, completing a checklist like the one in Appendix A will help remind students of the steps. Post the checklist in the classroom so students can refer to it frequently. As students become more skilled at the process, a written checklist may no longer be needed and may even become frustrating to students who have internalized the problem-solving process and are now focusing their attentions on other problem-solving skills. Stopping at each step to record their actions may distract them from the problem. Your knowledge of your students' abilities, gathered through constant monitoring and assessment, will help you recognize those students who will benefit from a step-by-step approach and those who will be more effective without the structured checklist. Providing a checklist for selected students similar to the one shown in Appendix A is a good way to address the different needs of the students in your classroom. Students can be asked to make notes on the checklist as they proceed through the steps of the process, or the checklist can be used to stimulate discussion among partners, teams, or the entire class. It serves to remind students of the steps in the problem-solving process.

Helping Students Get "Unstuck"

Students often become stuck when attempting to solve problems. When solutions are not immediately apparent, they can become frustrated and give up. Helping them learn ways to get themselves "unstuck" is an important lesson in their growth as problem solvers.

As students become stuck during classroom problem-solving experiences, teachers can guide them with suggestions and encouragement. It is especially important, however, that after the problem has been solved, students are asked to reflect on how they got "unstuck." Asking students what they did that proved successful and highlighting those effective strategies for continuing to move forward in the problem-solving process will benefit all students in the class as they share experiences and begin to develop a repertoire of strategies for those frustrating moments.

Following are some self-help strategies for getting "unstuck." Students might develop their own list of strategies based on their experiences and the experiences of their classmates. Similar ideas can be shared with parents during a parent night at school, as in Appendix I, providing them with ideas on how to guide their children through home problem-solving activities.

CLASSROOM-TESTED TIP

Problem-Solving Icons

As students attempt to select an appropriate strategy for solving a problem the use of icons can serve to remind them of the strategies they have explored in class. A bulletin board or special area of the classroom can be designated to display icons (pictures to represent the strategies). As students explore a specific strategy, an icon for that strategy, like the ones in Appendix F, is displayed. Additional icons are displayed as students build their repertoire of strategies. Throughout the year, as students attempt to solve problems, the teacher can direct their attention to the icons as reminders of possible solution strategies.

Jot Down Ideas

Jot down a plan for how you will be solving the problem. You might list the important information or draw a diagram of the problem to get you started.

Restate the Problem in Your Own Words

Are you unsure how to begin? Reread the problem and then state it in your own words. You need to understand the problem before you can go any further.

Cross Off Unnecessary Information

Is the problem confusing, containing too much data? Reread the problem and cross out the unnecessary data to simplify the problem.

Substitute with Simpler Numbers

Does the problem contain large numbers or fractions or decimals that are confusing you? Substitute simpler numbers for the confusing numbers and then figure out how to solve the problem. Once you know how the problem should be solved, just plug the more complicated numbers back into the problem and repeat the process to solve it.

Take a Break

Are you too frustrated to go on? Take a break for a few minutes. Think about or do something else. Then return to the problem refreshed and ready to begin again.

Use a Manipulative

Use everyday objects (paper clips, toothpicks, pennies) to represent the items in the problem. Act out the problem with the manipulatives.

Talk the Problem Through

Talk out loud to yourself or to someone else. Explain the problem and what you think you should do. Listen to yourself as you talk to see if what you say makes sense.

Think of a Similar Problem

Does this problem remind you of another that you've solved? How did you solve that one? Try that strategy. Does it work here?

Try a Different Strategy

What you're doing doesn't seem to be working. Try something else. Is there a different strategy that you think might work? Try it and see.

Give Yourself a Pep Talk

Think of a problem you solved by sticking with it. Remember a time when you were frustrated but kept on trying until you found the answer. Remind yourself that you can do it!

Involving Students in Instruction

Teaching problem-solving strategies is teaching students to think in an organized manner. It is the process of helping students recognize how logical and productive thinking works. To do this, you can use techniques such as think-alouds, cooperative learning activities, visual demonstrations, and hands-on practice. By transforming thinking from an abstract idea to a visible activity, you will keep students engaged in the lessons, strengthen their understanding, and help them gain the skills they need to become more organized thinkers.

Again, it is important that you model your thinking by speaking aloud to students as you proceed through demonstration problems together. By sharing examples of logical thinking and modeling thoughtful questions and reasonable conclusions, you will help highlight for students what should be happening in their own heads during the problem-solving process.

In addition, it is important that students have opportunities to discuss strategies with one another as they formulate and test ideas about how to proceed with each problem. Cooperative learning strategies are valuable tools during problem-solving instruction, as they allow students to hear others' thoughts and help each child expand his or her repertoire of ideas. Working with partners or groups gives students the opportunity to test their ideas on others or analyze their teammates' ideas and solutions. Group work helps students monitor their thinking, analyze their progress, and discuss alternate methods of solving each problem. Working with others also helps reduce the anxiety that often comes with "standing alone" and allows students to take risks and gain confidence in their own abilities. It allows them to practice their thinking in a safe and comfortable environment.

Visual and hands-on demonstrations are also critical in helping students understand problem-solving strategies. You can use an overhead projector, blackboard, or dry-erase board for demonstrations to help students visualize the strategy. Using hands-on materials to simulate a problem or create a diagram helps students re-create what is happening in the problem. As students develop an understanding of the strategy, the visual and hands-on examples will naturally give way to more abstract thinking.

Students need repeated practice with each strategy, and they need to be given opportunities to decide which strategies apply to which problems. After initial exposure to each strategy, the teacher should give students multiple opportunities to look at a mixed group of problems and determine which strategy makes sense in each situation. Students will often remember certain problems that serve as anchor problems. As students realize "That's just like the pizza problem!", they will begin to connect the new problem to the familiar "pizza" problem and recognize that applying the same strategy may be successful. During these types of activities, they need opportunities to hear others' ideas and discuss the appropriateness of specific strategies, because often more than one strategy may be effective.

And, connecting problem-solving instruction to real-world experiences and data helps students recognize the purpose for learning each strategy. Throughout this book, you will see an emphasis on using real-world problems during problem-solving instruction. During early instruction, problems should reflect the interests of the students and may deal with games, pets, or homework. As students become more adept at problem solving, they are better able to deal with the challenge of real data. Unlike textbook word problems, real-world problems are not always clear-cut, easily defined, and composed of simple numbers. Students are faced with making sense of real data as they attempt to solve the problem, which prepares them for future problem-solving experiences in a way that textbooks and worksheets are unable to do.

CHAPTER THREE

Assessing Problem Solving

Students' progress should be assessed systematically, deliberately, and continually to effectively influence students' confidence and ability to solve problems in various contexts. Giving students feedback about the results of this assessment, on both the processes used and the results attained, is critical to their development as problem solvers.   NCTM

The Role of Ongoing Assessment

Teachers have traditionally viewed assessment as a culminating activity, providing information about whether each student has mastered a unit's content. Fortunately, we are beginning to recognize that assessment can and should take place throughout the instructional process. Ongoing assessment allows us to gather information about students' learning and monitor students' progress. It also helps us make sound instructional decisions by identifying those skills and concepts that need to be retaught or modified to ensure success for all students. Rather than being a final wrap-up of what was learned, assessment should guide our instruction to ensure that we are on track with our instructional activities. For that reason, I address assessment early in this book. A thorough understanding of problem-solving assessment will guide you through the later chapters and help you plan solid instructional activities that specifically address your assessment outcomes.

Because of the value of ongoing assessment in guiding the instructional process, it is critical that assessment and instruction be developed hand in hand. Consider your mathematics outcomes as your travel destination. Without a clear view of your students' destination, it will be difficult to determine the path they should travel to get there. But, with expected student outcomes in mind, instructional activities can be designed to move your students in the direction of their destination. Frequent assessment activities will ensure that your students stay on the right path and will help redirect those students who might become lost along the way.

Whether an activity is an assessment activity or an instructional activity depends on the way it is administered and reviewed with students. During instruction, the teacher demonstrates and models activities. Students practice their skills under the guidance and direction of the teacher. During assessment, the teacher gives students opportunities to independently solve problems. Problem solving may happen in groups or individually, but it happens without teacher guidance. These independent tasks provide an idea of how each student is progressing in his or her skill development. They provide information that will be essential for planning subsequent classroom lessons or valuable to share during individual student or parent conferences. They allow you to analyze students' work for patterns in errors or misunderstandings of the concepts you've taught.

In assessing problem solving, attention should be paid to both the process and the product. When analyzing students' problem-solving abilities, two very helpful types of assessment are teacher observations of the problem-solving process and the evaluation of written, open-ended problem-solving tasks. Through analyzing both student behaviors and the products created during their problem-solving experiences, teachers can gather a wealth of information to assess students' problem-solving abilities and plan for future instruction.

Finally, it is important to recognize that what you think you have taught is not always what students have learned. Despite your belief that a concept was fully explained or a process was sufficiently modeled, if students are still confused, it is your responsibility to think of new ways to explain it until they have learned it. Ongoing assessment will help you determine when clarification, revision, or reteaching is appropriate.

The Value of Observations

Much information can be gained about students' understanding of the problem-solving process through classroom observations. As students solve problems in pairs or groups, teachers should circulate throughout the classroom, assessing students' understanding of the process. By listening to group discussions, teachers can gather valuable information regarding students' understanding of the problem, their ability to work together and share

ideas as they work toward a solution, and their ability to judge the reasonableness of both their plan and, ultimately, their solution. As students explain their ideas to other group members or challenge others' thinking, you will gather information about each student's level of expertise. These observations can be informal and used simply to get a general sense of class abilities, or they can be formal observations in which checklists are used to evaluate individual students or groups of students. Teacher-developed checklists will help you gather information on students' ability to collaborate, reason, and problem solve. Appendix C contains a sample group checklist.

Observation checklists may also be designed for individual student assessment. Checklist items might include whether a specific student contributed to the problem-solving activity, was able to restate a problem or explain a solution, or contributed a reasonable strategy to the group's discussion. Whether observations are formal or informal, they provide insight into students' understanding of the problem-solving process. Post-observation conferences with individuals or groups allow you to discuss your observations with students and help them see the value of collaborative problem solving.

The Value of Rubrics in Assessment

Written assessment tasks provide information on individual students' problem-solving abilities. While multiple-choice tests are appropriate in many mathematical situations, open-ended assignments provide much more information when assessing problem solving. Students' responses to open-ended problem situations will provide you with valuable information about their level of understanding of the problem-solving process.

To be most effective for you and your students, scoring keys should be developed before instruction takes place. In this way, you can focus on what you want students to learn and then design instructional tasks that will get them there. A general scoring key that can be applied to a set of activities is called a *rubric*. The use of rubrics to assess problem-solving activities offers students a chance to see what is expected of them before they begin a problem-solving task. It can help guide them as they work through a problem, reminding them of the important points to consider in solving the problem. After their task is scored, it allows them to see the degree to which they were able to meet the assessment criteria, and therefore, it becomes a valuable tool in helping them understand how they can improve their work.

Rubrics can be holistic (assessing the students' ability to perform the task as a whole) or analytic (assessing the degree to which students demonstrate their proficiency on a specific outcome). The type of rubric you choose will depend on the assessment information you wish to gain.

A Holistic Rubric for Problem Solving

A holistic rubric rates the student's ability to complete a task that is a compilation of several outcomes. Problem solving is such a task. There are several key outcomes that you should look for when assessing students' problem-solving skills.

First, students should be able to select and use an appropriate strategy. Not all students will select the same strategy, but each selection should make sense as a means to solve the problem (see Figures 3–1 and 3–2).

Second, students should be able to find a correct solution. There may be more than one correct solution. Students' solutions need to make sense with the data they have at hand. In addition, students' answers need to be the result of correct calculations.

Third, students need to be able to communicate about their problem solving. Your students' abilities to communicate their thoughts about solving problems will give you a clearer picture of each student's level of knowledge. Their writing offers insight into the process they went through to arrive at

FIGURE 3–1

their answer. It often provides information about which you might otherwise need to conjecture. In light of the strong emphasis of the NCTM Standards regarding the development of mathematical communication, it is recommended that writing be integrated into the problem-solving process and become a part of your holistic rubric.

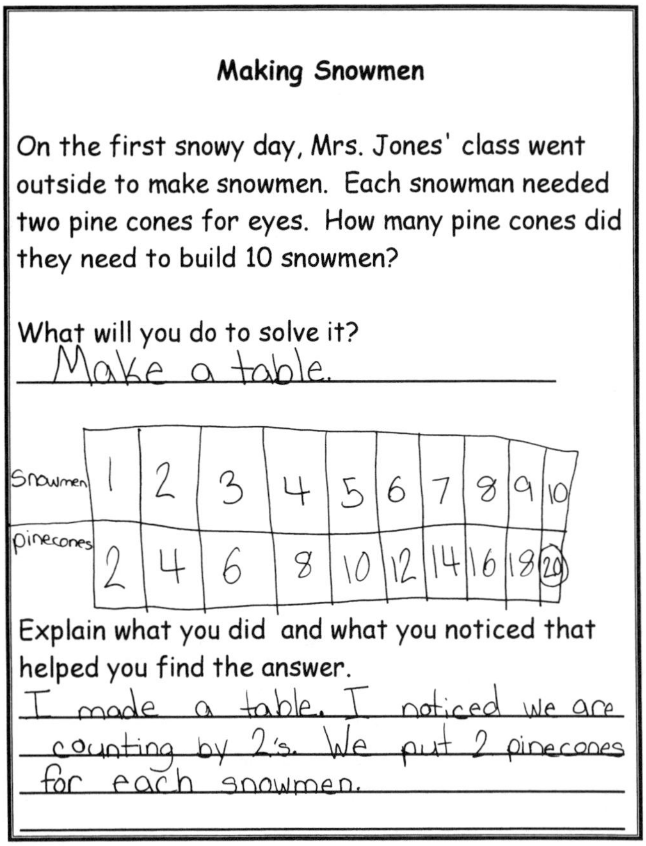

Once teachers have set outcomes for their students, developing a problem-solving rubric becomes easy. As students look at their completed problems, they are able to see the outcomes they have met and those that they have not yet mastered. With this information in mind, they become able to revise their work to move closer to exemplary-quality work.

Figure 3–3 is a holistic rubric for problem-solving activities. First, the rubric lists the expected student outcomes, then it outlines the criteria needed to earn scores ranging from 0–4.

Making Snowmen

On the first snowy day, Mrs. Jones' class went outside to make snowmen. Each snowman needed two pine cones for eyes. How many pine cones did they need to build 10 snowmen? *20 pinecones*

What will you do to solve it?
I will use a diagram.

ⓒ ⓒ ⓒ ⓒ ⓒ ⓒ ⓒ ⓒ ⓒ ⓒ

Explain what you did, and what you noticed that helped you find the answer.
I drew the ten heads and then drew the eyes. What helped me was the eyes because I could count them.

FIGURE 3–2 These second-grade students selected different strategies for solving the problem. Both strategies are appropriate and guided the students to the correct solution.

Expected Student Outcomes:

Students will be able to

1. select and use an appropriate strategy.

2. calculate a correct answer.

3. explain their strategy for solving the problem.

Problem-Solving Rubric:

4–arrived at a correct answer; used an appropriate strategy; adequately explained answer

3–used an appropriate strategy; calculated a correct answer but was unable to explain the strategy; *or* adequately explained the strategy but did not calculate a correct answer

2–used an appropriate strategy; did not find a correct answer; could not explain the strategy

1–attempted to solve the problem, but completely incorrect in attempt

0–no attempt/blank

FIGURE 3–3 Rubrics are designed with expected student outcomes in mind.

This rubric offers a quick and easy way to assess your students' ability to solve problems. In this rubric, the selection of a strategy, the calculation of an answer, and the written explanation of the answer are the expected student outcomes. The ultimate goal is that students be able to meet all three outcomes as a demonstration of their problem-solving skills. Students who have seen the rubric prior to the activity will be focused on these three important outcomes that they are expected to demonstrate. In this way, the rubric helps guide students through the problem-solving experience.

In order to score a 2 or higher, students must demonstrate their ability to select and use an appropriate strategy. Selecting a reasonable strategy is the foundation for good problem solving. If a student lacks the abil-ity to think through a situation and decide on a plan for solving the problem, his or her correct answer may be no more than a lucky guess. Students who are able to find a correct answer based on an appropriate strategy and explain the strategy they selected will receive higher scores to correlate with their greater ability to complete the problem-solving task.

While the first two expected outcomes will always remain the same, the final outcome may be reworded to direct students to different types of mathematical communication. Some examples might include justifying the solution or explaining why a particular strategy was used. In each case, the outcome of strengthening mathematical communication is addressed with a slightly different writing assignment.

The Role of Rubrics in Improvement

The rubric is an effective tool for guiding students in revising their problem solving. Many teachers allow students to rewrite responses after the initial scoring. This technique encourages students to focus on the rubric and attempt to improve their writing and increase their score. Much like a revision checklist helps students polish a written composition in language arts class, the rubric guides students in their mathematical revision process (see Figure 3–4 and 3–5).

An evaluation worksheet like the sample in Appendix D will direct students through an analysis of their work. As students review their own work with the rubric in mind, they

Lunchables

Oscar Mayer*Lunchables are your favorite lunch and they are on sale! You can buy 3 packages for $5.00. How many Lunchables can you buy for $15.00? Complete the table to help you solve the problem.

Lunchables	3	6	⑨	12	15	18
Dollars	5	10	15	20	25	30

Circle your answer on the table.

Look for patterns on the table. Describe one of the patterns you see.

I see that your adding three to each number on the top row and on the bottom your adding 5 to each number.

FIGURE 3–5   After another look at the rubric and some classroom discussion, this student revised his work. This time, he was able to correctly address all of the outcomes and scored a 4.
*OSCAR Mayer is a registered trademark of Kraft Foods, Inc. and is used with permission.

are able to see ways in which they can improve. The ability of students to analyze and improve their own work is our ultimate goal, as it indicates that students have internalized the strategies we have taught.

Analytic Rubrics for Assessing Specific Skills

While with the holistic rubric, the goal is to have students demonstrate their ability to perform all three outcomes in order to successfully complete the task, the analytic rubric looks in more detail at the degree to which one outcome has been mastered. Analytic rubrics assess the degree of correctness or completeness of students' calculations or responses. With this type of rubric, each of our problem-solving outcomes—students'

Lunchables

Oscar Mayer*Lunchables are your favorite lunch and they are on sale! You can buy 3 packages for $5.00. How many Lunchables can you buy for $15.00? Complete the table to help you solve the problem.

Lunchables	3	6	9	12	15	18
Dollars	5	10	15	20	25	30

Circle your answer on the table.

Look for patterns on the table. Describe one of the patterns you see.

One of the patterns I see is on the top row the numbers are odd then even all the way down.

FIGURE 3–4   On first attempt, this student used an appropriate strategy—making tables—but was not able to correctly locate the answer from the table. In addition, the student was not able to describe one of the patterns on the table. Using a holistic rubric, the teacher gave this student a score of 2.
*OSCAR Mayer is a registered trademark of Kraft Foods, Inc. and is used with permission.

ability to select and use an appropriate strategy, students' ability to calculate a correct answer, and students' ability to explain their thinking—can be judged individually as to the degree to which the student has mastered it. This type of rubric is valuable in that it allows you to identify specific strengths and weaknesses. You are then able to address weaknesses with additional instruction.

Outcome 1: Select and Use an Appropriate Strategy

An important problem-solving skill is the ability to identify and use an appropriate strategy. It is not necessary that the student select the same strategy that you had in mind when designing the problem. Remember the different strategies selected by the second graders in Figure 3–1 and 3–2. For each problem, you must look at a student's work and determine the reasonableness of the strategy that he or she selected. The degree to which the student can carry out the selected strategy can be assessed with the analytic rubric in Figure 3–6.

Outcome 2: Calculate a Correct Answer

Calculating the correct answer is an important part of the problem-solving process.

Often, calculations require several operations and students can make small errors, despite showing the evidence that they understand the arithmetic operations that would lead to a correct answer. At other times, students appear to be confused from the start and make multiple errors in calculating an answer. If you use the rubric shown in Figure 3–7 when assessing a student's ability to correctly calculate an answer, you will gather valuable information about the student's skills. *Note:* There are some problem-solving strategies for which this rubric would not be applicable. For example, if students are drawing a picture or diagram to solve a problem, no calculations may be necessary.

Outcome 3: Communicate Mathematically

When you learn to teach students how to explain their work or justify their solutions in writing, using a rubric that addresses only the explanation part of the answer will help them improve their communication skills. Developing good writing skills requires practice on the part of your students. A rubric like the one in Figure 3–8 will help them see the components of a well-written response.

Expected Student Outcome:

Students will be able to select and use an appropriate problem-solving strategy.

Rubric for Selecting an Appropriate Strategy:

4 – reasonable strategy selected and fully developed, including diagrams or labeled work to support the strategy

3 – reasonable strategy selected; moderately developed

2 – reasonable strategy selected, but minimally developed; major errors may be evident

1 – strategy choice is inappropriate for problem

0 – no attempt/blank

FIGURE 3–6   This rubric assesses a student's ability to select an appropriate problem-solving strategy.

Expected Student Outcome:

Students will be able to correctly calculate the answer to the problem.

Calculation Rubric:

4 – calculations are completely correct and answers are properly labeled

3 – calculations are mostly correct; minor errors may occur

2 – calculations contain major errors

1 – calculations are completely incorrect

0 – no attempt/blank

FIGURE 3–7   This rubric assesses a student's ability to correctly calculate an answer.

Expected Student Outcome:

Students will be able to clearly explain the strategy they used to solve the problem.

Mathematical Communication Rubric:

4 – exemplary explanation; detailed and clear; may have provided examples

3 – explanation contained adequate details; adequate clarity

2 – explanation somewhat clear; lacks details

1 – attempted an explanation, but incorrect or unclear

0 – no attempt/blank

FIGURE 3–8 This rubric assesses a student's ability to communicate mathematical ideas.

The responses to the following problem illustrate the varying degrees to which students might demonstrate their ability to communicate mathematically.

SAMPLE PROBLEM:

For the school cupcake sale, parents made chocolate, yellow, and lemon cupcakes. They iced them with chocolate, vanilla, and swirl icing. How many different cake and icing combinations are possible?

Question: How can you be sure you listed **every possible combination?**

Score–4

"I got my answer by listing out my choices. First I wrote down the first kind of cake and wrote all the icing choices with it. Then I crossed out chocolate cake and went to yellow cake and did the same thing. Then I crossed out yellow in the problem and went to lemon. I continued until I crossed out all the cake choices. I had chocolate with chocolate, chocolate with vanilla, and chocolate with swirl. Then I had yellow with chocolate, yellow with vanilla, and yellow with swirl. Then I had lemon with chocolate, lemon with vanilla, and lemon with swirl. I did them in order so I wouldn't miss any."

This student clearly explained how he made a list using each type of cupcake and each type of icing. He gave examples to support his thinking. He mentioned the importance of making his list in an organized way and indicated that he crossed off items after he exhausted them on his list.

Score–3

"I listed each kind of icing under each kind of cupcake, so I can be sure I got all of the combinations."

This student understood that the goal was to list each type of cupcake and then each kind of icing until all possibilities were used. The explanation is brief but correct and adequate.

Score–2

"I put all the cupcakes and icings together."

This student's response lacks clarity. He mentions "all" the cupcakes and icings, so he may have the idea, but it is unclear whether the student used the strategy correctly. This student needs to explain in more detail.

Score–1

"I know I listed possible combinations because I have seen and tasted these combinations that I listed.

This student's response addresses the question about possible combinations, but does not answer the question. An attempt was made.

Score–0
blank

This student did not attempt to answer the question.

You can assist students in strengthening their problem-solving abilities and developing their writing skills in several ways. Think-alouds that model well-developed explanations provide students with examples of logical thinking. Discussions among partners or groups, during which students can share their ideas, help students develop a variety of ways to explain their thinking process.

Problem solving is a thinking skill. In order to monitor how students' thinking is

---

CLASSROOM-TESTED TIP

Using Rubrics to Improve Mathematical Communication Skills

One way to help students see the degree to which an explanation is clear and detailed is to evaluate writing samples as a class. Write several responses of your own, with varying degrees of clarity, and have students score them using the rubric. Students can use an all-pupil response method such as raising the number of fingers to show the score they would give each writing sample or pinching a number from 0 to 4 on a pinch card (a card showing numbers on both sides, so the student and the teacher can see the student's choice) to indicate their choice of scores. (See Appendix E.) As students give a score to the writing sample, have them justify the score using the criteria in the scoring key. Together, the class can rewrite the sample to give it a higher score.

Another technique that helps students learn to use a rubric to guide revision is compiling a list of responses with scores of 1, 2, 3, and 4. In pairs or groups, the students discuss and evaluate the differences between the writing samples and attempt to determine what is missing in the responses that scored 1, 2, and 3. Together, each group works to rewrite the 1 to make it a 2, the 2 to make it a 3, or the 3 to make it a 4. Groups can then present their revised writing to the class.

Showing students concrete examples of how to improve their writing with details, examples, and clarity of thought will help them strengthen their skills in this area.

---

progressing, it is important to frequently ask students to share their thoughts both orally and in writing. Students' writing allows you to recognize difficulties or misunderstandings they might be experiencing. It offers a valuable glimpse into their thinking processes and allows you to determine if they are progressing smoothly in their understanding of the problem-solving process.

Self-Reflections on Problem Solving

Teachers should offer students opportunities to reflect on their problem solving through journal writing, allowing them to express their successes and frustrations as they develop as problem solvers. Problem-solving journals that allow students to reflect on daily or weekly lessons provide teachers with insight into their students' perceptions, confusions, and successes. Ideas for open-ended journal writing prompts are included in Appendix D. Journal writing should not be scored, although teacher comments are recommended. Teacher

and student can often begin a dialogue through journal writing in which the teacher encourages the student and points out the student's growth and successes.

Varied Assessment

Both holistic and analytic rubrics are valuable ways to analyze students' progress. Whether you are assessing students' ability to put together the needed skills to effectively solve problems (holistic rubrics) or analyzing strengths and weaknesses in a specific outcome area (analytic rubrics), a great deal of information can be gained from frequent assessment. Teacher observations and student self-reflections also contribute important data to the assessment process. Ongoing and varied assessment throughout the teaching process will provide the information you need to make strong instructional decisions and, ultimately, create a classroom filled with successful problem solvers.

CHAPTER FOUR

Strategy: Choose an Operation

Understanding the fundamental operations of addition, subtraction, multiplication, and division is central to knowing mathematics. One essential component of what it means to understand an operation is recognizing conditions in real-world situations that indicate that the operation would be useful in those situations.   NCTM

Addition, subtraction, multiplication, and division are methods of finding the solution to many math problems. Determining which of these operations is appropriate for solving a problem is a critical, and very common, problem-solving strategy.

Students' ability to select the correct operation when solving word problems can often be a reflection of the way in which they were taught each operation. Students who memorized math facts without developing a clear understanding of the concepts may have more difficulty identifying when each operation should be used than those students who developed an understanding of each concept through demonstrations, explanations, and hands-on experiences. In the initial teaching of each operation, it is imperative that students understand the concept of when to use that operation. When students begin to learn about multiplication, for example, it is important that they see and hear situations in which

groups of equal size are put together to form a larger group. After seeing and hearing about the concept repeatedly, students are able to understand the operation involved in 3×4, rather than just knowing that the answer is 12 because of repeated flash card practice.

Key Words Versus Key Concepts

Although teachers often use key words as a method of assisting students in choosing an appropriate operation, be careful about teaching students to rely solely on key words. It is often true that when the phrase *less than* appears in a problem, it is a subtraction problem. Those words, however, can appear in other problems, and students who look for one or two familiar words but do not stop to analyze the entire problem may incorrectly determine that subtraction is the operation to use. Particularly with the increase in real-world problem-solving tasks and more complex performance tasks, there may be several key words within a problem that will mislead the student who is relying only on key words.

Students should look for key concepts rather than key words. After reading the problem, they should try to make sense of the situation rather than focusing on a word or phrase in hopes that it will tell them how to proceed. Understanding the key concepts for each operation will help students make a thoughtful decision regarding the appropriate operation to use in solving the problem.

Practice with Recognizing Key Concepts

Addition
Addition is the process of putting things together. The sets do not need to be equal. The key word *altogether* is often used—just be cautioned that it is the *concept* of altogether (bringing groups together), not the word, that tells a student that it is time to add. If you are trying to find out the total number of students who are wearing red today, you add the five students wearing red shoes to the three students wearing red shirts to the six students wearing red socks to find the answer.

Addition is an appropriate operation to use to find out the total number of items even if each group is equal. If we are trying to decide the total number of cookies on the table, and there are four plates with seven cookies on each of them, we can find it by adding 7 + 7 + 7 + 7, although multiplication is a faster way to find the answer for students who have learned that operation. Placing groups of objects on the overhead and physically pulling them together will illustrate this concept. Physical demonstrations in the classroom with groups of students or the use of desktop manipulatives to illustrate addition problems will help students see the objects coming together as a whole group.

Subtraction
Subtraction is more difficult for students to understand because there are several models for subtraction. The first, and easiest, is the "take-away" model. Whenever you remove

something from a group, you subtract. Students pick this concept up very quickly. If there were five frogs on lily pads and three jumped into the water, subtraction would help you find out how many frogs were left on lily pads. Another very important model for subtraction is the "compare" model. Whenever items are compared, you use subtraction to find the difference between them. If you are asking students to determine how much one object is taller, wider, or heavier than another, they would subtract to find the answer. Reminding students that whenever they compare, they should subtract will help them master this concept. Another phrase often used in subtraction problems asks a child to determine how many more of something are needed to make two items equal. This is a form of comparison. For example, a comparison problem could read: **If Katie had 16 baseball cards and Michael had 7 baseball cards, how many more cards would Michael need to buy to have the same number as Katie?** Using overhead counters and lining up the two rows next to each other to allow students to see the difference between the two groups will help them visualize this comparison model.

Multiplication
The concept of multiplication can be easily demonstrated with real objects, manipulatives, or overhead materials. Like addition, multiplication is used to find the total number of objects; however, when using multiplication, all sets *must* have the same number of objects. If there are six teams for physical education class, and each team has five students, multiplication can be used to find the total number of students in physical education. Using manipulatives to construct equal groups and then pulling the groups together on an overhead or on students' desktops will visually demonstrate the concept of multiplication.

Division
Division is an operation about which students often become confused. Many students confuse subtraction and division. Again, a visual representation will help students see that you

are starting with a large group and then splitting that group into smaller groups. No objects are disappearing from the group, as in the take-away model of subtraction. Division asks how many smaller groups are formed or how many items are in each smaller group.

Posters or signs in the classroom can help remind students of the key concepts for each operation as in Appendix B. It is important to remind students that it is not the key words that indicate which operation to use, but the key concepts. We are not looking for the word *altogether*, because it will not appear in all problems. We are looking for the *concept* of putting things together. When students are able to identify the concept, they will be able to successfully choose the appropriate operation.

Practice with Choosing the Correct Operation

Group Activities and Discussions

It is important for students to have opportunities to practice selecting the appropriate operation. This can be done through pair and group activities in which students are given a team problem and asked to determine the correct operation. As students discuss which operation they would choose and why, they hear one another's ideas and strengthen their understanding of the key concepts. When sharing their answers with the rest of the class, students should always include a justification for their choice of operations, telling *why* they chose the operation they did.

Pinch Cards

Pinch cards, a form of all-pupil response, also provide practice in identifying the correct operation. All students receive their own card. Primary students would work with a card that has addition and subtraction, while older students would work with a card that includes all four operations. Teachers can create their own cards, being sure to duplicate the card on both sides of the paper, or use the samples in Appendix E. The operation signs should be placed in the same location on the front and back of the card, so students can see the sign from the back of the card while teachers see the same sign from the front. As the teacher

---

CLASSROOM-TESTED TIP

Hands-On Introductions to Subtraction and Division

As you demonstrate the take-away model for subtraction using the overhead projector, it is helpful to mark a circle on the overhead and place the original group inside the circle. As you take away, students will see you remove the objects from the circle but will still see them on the screen. They are then able to count how many have been taken from the group and how many still remain.

As you demonstrate division, again draw a circle and place the whole group in the circle. As the group is divided, each subgroup will remain in the circle. Students will see that no objects leave the circle; the group is only rearranged into smaller groups.

Subtraction

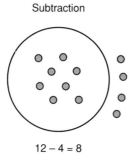

12 − 4 = 8

Division

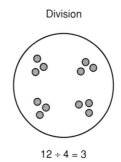

12 ÷ 4 = 3

poses a problem, students pinch (hold the card by the sign) the operation they would use to solve the problem. This allows a quick, interactive review that students enjoy, and it allows you to quickly spot those students who are still having difficulty with the concepts. Those students may be pulled aside later for review or reteaching.

Student-Created Problems

Asking students to develop their own problems related to sets of data is another way to help them strengthen their skills at understanding the operations. Give students a set of data and ask them to create a real problem that might use the data. For example, students may write a variety of problems using the following data.

Data: 8 slices of pizza, $1.50 per slice of pizza, 4 children

Sample student-created problems include:

"There were 8 slices of pizza and 4 children. If they shared equally, how many pieces would each child get?"

"The children bought 8 slices of pizza. Each slice costs $1.50. How much did they spend?"

"Three children had one slice of pizza each. The other child ate the rest. How many slices did he eat?"

"One child bought a slice of pizza and paid with a $5.00 bill. How much change did he get back?"

"Kathy had a $5.00 bill. How many slices of pizza could she buy?"

After students write their story problems, have them present the problems to their group or the entire class. Students can trade problems between partners or groups and solve one another's problems. Students might be asked to sort the problems by operation. Be sure to ask them to explain how they knew which operation they should use to solve each problem. Some of the student-written problems might be used for class problem-solving warm-ups over the next few days.

CLASSROOM-TESTED TIP

Writing Story Problems

Using equations to prompt students to write story problems is an effective way to assess students' understanding of the basic operations. Provide students with an equation and ask them to create a story problem to match the equation. Consider the following equation: 10 + 21 = 31

Story: *Katie bought some candy. She bought 10 chocolate kisses and 21 peppermints. How many pieces of candy did she buy altogether?*

There are lots of other stories that might go with the same equation.

Another story: *There were 10 daisies and 21 roses in Mrs. Alexander's garden. How many flowers were in her garden?*

Students can write their stories in math journals or share their stories aloud with their group or the whole class. With a thumbs-up/thumbs-down response, classmates can evaluate the stories to see if they match the equation. If stories don't match the equation, classmates can suggest ways to rewrite the story to make it fit. Writing story problems helps students strengthen their understanding of the operations.

A variation of this activity is to put students in pairs and give each student a different equation on an index card. Ask students to turn over the index card so their partners cannot see it. Ask each student to write a story for their equation. When students have finished, have them switch stories with their partners. After reading their partner's story, students must figure out the equation.

A Look at Student Work

The following samples of student writing help to illustrate students' reasoning regarding choosing an appropriate operation. In each case, students have analyzed the problem situation and chosen the operation based on their understanding of the problem, not their recognition of key words that appear in the problem.

Students were asked to sell raffle tickets for the school Fun Fair. Ryan sold 5 tickets to his mother, 7 tickets to his father, and 3 tickets to his grandmother. How many tickets did Ryan sell?

"I added because Ryan wants to see how many he sold to all three people, which means he wants to put them together."

In the long jump event, Steven's jump measured 173 centimeters. Melissa jumped 164 centimeters. How many more centimeters would Melissa have had to jump to tie Steven?

"I used subtraction because you need to subtract in order to find the difference between 173 and 164. That's the same number of centimeters more that Melissa would have had to jump in order for there to be a tie." (Notice the idea of comparison!)

Mrs. Singer's students were working in teams for math class. There were 4 students in each team. Mrs. Singer had 7 teams of students in her classroom. How many students were in Mrs. Singer's class?

"I multiplied to find out how many because every team had the same number and when that happens you can multiply and it's faster than adding."

There were 132 students participating in Field Day. The students were split into 12 equal teams. How many students were on each team?

"I chose to divide because when you divide you split things into even groups and that's what I needed to do to solve this problem."

Reflecting on the Strategy

Asking students to explain how and why they arrived at an answer or selected an operation will help you better assess their understanding of the operations. Allowing students to work in pairs or groups to discuss their choice of operations will help them begin to develop ways to verbalize their thoughts. By listening to others and sharing ideas, they will acquire the vocabulary they need to explain their mathematical thinking. Young students may do some of their "explaining" through pictures or diagrams, but even in early grades it is important to encourage students to put their thoughts in writing, both to help them solidify their own knowledge and to help you better assess their skills.

Selecting Practice Problems

Practice problems using addition, subtraction, multiplication, and division are available in any math book. Keep in mind, however, that real-world problems will help students connect the math skills they are learning to events and situations in their own lives. Problems that relate to students will motivate and excite them. Simple activities like rewording textbook problems to include your students' names or the names of local restaurants, parks, or schools will help to personalize the problem-solving experience. Using data from local menus, travel brochures, or baseball cards will keep students involved in your lessons and demonstrate the meaningfulness of the mathematics skills they are learning. Seize any opportunity to make a real-world connection for your students. (Real-world problem solving is explored more fully in Chapter Twelve.)

CHAPTER FIVE

Strategy: Find a Pattern

By continuing to provide a broad variety of opportunities to explore and use patterns, we help students move from a basic recognition of patterns to a more sophisticated use of patterns as a problem-solving strategy.   Terrence G. Coburn

Patterns are an important part of our number system. Students begin to recognize and repeat patterns early in their mathematics education. This ability to understand, recognize, and extend patterns helps students solve many math problems.

In primary grades, students begin to investigate patterns through hands-on experiences. Teachers create patterns for students to echo such as snap–clap–snap–clap. Students make real patterns as they sit, sit, stand, sit, sit, stand. Students work with color cubes to create color patterns like blue–green–green–blue–green–green. As students internalize the concept that patterns repeat in a predictable way, they become able to continue the patterns.

In much the same way, students begin to see patterns within our number system. As they skip count in primary grades, they begin to recognize the way the numbers repeat and are then able to predict which number comes next. Directing students to take a closer look

at patterns in numbers will assist them in drawing some interesting conclusions.

10, 20, 30, 40 . . .

"It's like counting 1, 2, 3, 4 and putting a zero behind each number."

5, 10, 15, 20 . . .

"First they end with a 5 and then they end with a 0."

Discovering a Variety of Patterns

Patterns range from simple to very complex. Red–blue, red–blue, red–blue is a simple *ab* pattern. Red–red–blue, red–red–blue, red–red–blue is an example of an *aab* pattern. Patterns can also be growing patterns like the following: 1–2, 1–2–2, 1–2–2–2. . . . Giving students a chance to see a variety of patterns will help them become more sophisticated at recognizing and extending them. As students become skilled at simpler patterns, challenge them with growing patterns or patterns that have two attributes like the different letters and sizes in the following pattern: XxOoXx OoXxOo . . . . An even more challenging pattern can be created by incorporating a growing pattern into a letter/size pattern as in xoxo, XOXO, xxooxxoo, XXOOXXOO, xxxooxxxooo, XXXOOOXXXOOO . . . . Continue to challenge your students with patterns of increasing complexity.

Completing and Describing Number Patterns

Challenging students with more complex number patterns will help focus them on the variety of patterns that can be created. If you

ask students to describe patterns, it will help you analyze their understanding of the patterns.

2, 4, 8, 16 . . .
"You doubled the number each time."

1, 3, 6, 10 . . .
"First you added one, then two, then three, then four."

2, 1, 3, 2, 4, 3 . . .
"I add two then take away one."

1, 2, 3, 5, 8 . . .
"I added the first two numbers to get the next one. I kept adding the last two numbers to get the next one."

CLASSROOM-TESTED TIP

Introducing Patterns Using Hundred Charts

A hundred chart can be a useful tool in helping students visualize number patterns (see Appendix G). As students begin to explore patterns by coloring in the squares on the chart, they see the patterns come to life. By coloring in the squares for the following pattern, students are able to visualize the pattern and predict which square will be colored in next: 3, 6, 9, 12 . . . .

1	2	3	4	5	6	7	8	9	10
11	12	13	14	15	16	17	18	19	20
21	22	23	24	25	26	27	28	29	30
31	32	33	34	35	36	37	38	39	49
41	42	43	44	45	46	47	48	49	50
51	52	53	54	55	56	57	58	59	60
61	62	63	64	65	66	67	68	69	70
71	72	73	74	75	76	77	78	79	80
81	82	83	84	85	86	87	88	89	90
91	92	93	94	95	96	97	98	99	100

Asking students to describe the pattern they have created will help strengthen their observation and communication skills.

"I skipped two squares and then I colored one and then I skipped two and then I colored one and then I skipped two and then I colored one, then I did it again. I should skip two and then color number 15."

Provide students with hundred chart demonstrations on an overhead transparency or poster-size chart to allow them to visualize our number system as a system of patterns. Even older students will be amazed at the patterns that can be created when coloring hundred charts. These patterns help to assure students of the predictability of our number system.

CLASSROOM-TESTED TIP

Hundred Chart Patterns

Have students work in pairs or groups to color in a hundred chart for multiples of 2, 3, 4, 5, 6, 7, 8, and 9. Ask them to work together to write a description of the pattern that their group created. Have them share their pattern with the class. Ask the class to compare the charts: How are they alike? How are they different?

Ask students to color in another chart for independent work. They may pick the criteria. Some ideas include:

- Two-digit numbers that end in 7
- Two-digit numbers that add up to 6

- Odd numbers
- Two-digit numbers that are only different by one digit (*e.g. 23, 32, 34, 43. . .*)
- Two-digit numbers that have two of the same digit
- Numbers where at least one of the digits is a 3

Encourage students to be creative. Display the completed hundred charts. Be sure to have students describe their patterns. (Hundred chart activities adapted from *About Teaching Mathematics* by Marilyn Burns.)

Working with Geometric Patterns

Patterns also exist in the geometric world. As students study shapes and chart sides and angles, they begin to recognize patterns. Take for example the following diagonal problem: **Can you predict how many diagonals can be made in an eight-sided figure?** Students can solve the problem by creating the figure and drawing the diagonals, but they can also solve the problem with an understanding of patterns. After students have drawn a few shapes and counted the diagonals, they will be able to predict the number of diagonals for the remaining shapes based on the pattern they have created.

Sides	4	5	6	7	8
Diagonals	2	5	9	14	

"I see a pattern. First you added three, then you added four, then you added five. I think you add one more each time. So I would add six this time. My answer is 20 diagonals."

CLASSROOM-TESTED TIP

Exploring Patterns with the Calculator

Students enjoy exploring patterns using the calculator's constant function. Students can command the calculator to add 3 or add 6 or multiply by 4 and then watch the calculator extend the pattern. For addition patterns, have students clear their calculators and press the addition sign, then the number they want added each time, for example, 2, and then press the equal sign. Each time the equal sign is pressed, the calculator will add 2. (⊞②⊟⊟⊟⊟) Students can count along as the pattern unfolds. When trying a subtraction pattern, first have students enter a number, say, 100, then a subtraction sign, then the number they want to subtract each time, such as 5. Each time they press the equal sign, the calculator will subtract five. (⒑⊟⑤⊟⊟⊟) For multiplication, students must first enter the number they want to multiply by and then the equal sign. For example, if they are doubling numbers, they will enter ②✕⊟⊟⊟⊟⊟⊟. With each equal sign that is entered, the numbers will double. You might ask students to predict how many times they would need to press the ⊟ key to get to a number that is greater than 100,000. Students will be amazed at how quickly this pattern will lead to very large numbers.

As drawing the figures becomes more difficult, say in the case of an eighteen-sided figure, the use of patterns becomes the preferred—and simpler—way to solve the problem.

A Look at Student Work

As students read and analyze problems, they often recognize a pattern within the data. Recognizing and being able to extend the pattern may lead to a solution, as in the example from a second-grade student shown in Figure 5–1. As the student describes the strategy she used to solve the problem, she relates how easy the problem was to solve because she only had to continue a pattern.

Figures 5–2 and 5–3 are examples of different ways in which fourth-grade students recorded their data in order to visualize the pattern. Both students were presented with

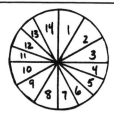

Spin the Wheel

At the school carnival, there was a prize wheel. Each student got to spin the wheel one time to see if they won a prize. Spinning a "one" won a prize. Spinning a "two" or "three" did not win anything. Spinning a "four" won a prize. Spinning a "five" or "six" did not win anything. Spinning a "seven" won a prize. Rita spun a 12. Did she win a prize? Explain how you figured out the answer.

Prize	no Prize
1	2, 3
4	5, 6
7	8, 9
10	11, 12

no Rita did not win a prize.

Explontion:
Rita did not win a prize because she spun a 12. If you follow the patter you can figure it out. I wrote prize, no prize and 12 landed on no prize.

FIGURE 5–2 This student sorts data into columns in order to analyze it.

the same problem, but each chose to record his or her data in a different, yet equally organized, way.

Simply extending a pattern does not always reveal the answer to a problem. In the problem shown in Figure 5–4, the student had to recognize the pattern and extend it and then had to add all of the figures to determine the total race time. Her understanding of patterns helped her compile the needed data so she could find the solution.

Reflecting on the Strategy

Asking students to write or talk about creating or extending patterns is a great way to assess students' understanding of patterns. Try prompts like these:

▮ Describe the pattern.

▮ If a new student entered the room who did not know anything about patterns,

---

Soccer Practice

Katie's soccer coach was trying to get the team in shape for the season. On the first day of practice, she made them run one lap around the field. On the second day, she made them run three laps. On the third day, they ran five laps, and on the fourth day they ran seven laps. How many laps did the coach make them run on the fifth day of practice?

They ran __9__ laps.   1, 3, 5, 7, 9

Describe the pattern. The patern was counting by two's.

How did knowing the pattern help you solve the problem? Knowing the pattern did help me. It was not so hard to do it because I knew how to count by two's.

FIGURE 5–1 Recognizing and extending patterns helps students solve problems.

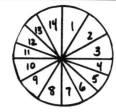

Spin the Wheel

At the school carnival, there was a prize wheel. Each student got to spin the wheel one time to see if they won a prize. Spinning a "one" won a prize. Spinning a "two" or "three" did not win anything. Spinning a "four" won a prize. Spinning a "five" or "six" did not win anything. Spinning a "seven" won a prize. Rita spun a 12. Did she win a prize? Explain how you figured out the answer.

Example

①23④56⑦89⑩ 11 12

No she did not. I found my anser by knowing the first number (1) wins and the next two don't. And then the number after the two wins and the next two numbers dont and so on. I followed this pattern all the way to 12 and found out that 12 closint win!

FIGURE 5–3   This student circles significant data to look for a pattern.

The Race

Andrew ran a six mile race. He ran the first mile in seven minutes. The second mile took him 7 1/2 minutes to run. He ran the third mile in 8 minutes, and the fourth mile in 8 1/2 minutes. Use the pattern to help you figure out how long it took him to complete the entire race.

$$7 + 7\frac{1}{2} + 8 + 8\frac{1}{2} + 9 + 9\frac{1}{2}$$

Andrew ran the entire race in 49 minutes, 30 seconds.

Describe the pattern in the problem. The pattern shows every mile, the minutes go up (30 seconds.)

How did knowing the pattern help you figure out the answer? Knowing the pattern helped me figure out the answer because every time a mile passed, it took an extra 30 seconds, and you had to add on the seconds and minutes. I found it out by adding 7:00 + 7:30 + 8:00 + 8:30 + 9:00 + 9:30 which equals 49 minutes 30 seconds.

FIGURE 5–4   In this problem, recognizing the pattern provided the student with the data needed to solve the problem.

- how would you explain what they are and how they can help you solve problems?
- Explain how understanding patterns helped you solve this problem.

- Is solving problems using patterns easy or hard? Explain your answer.

CHAPTER SIX

Strategy: Make a Table

Organizing data in a table is an essential mathematical skill. It helps

children to see relationships within patterns and eventually to

generalize these relationships to form a rule.   Terrence G. Coburn

One strategy that assists students in organizing data to solve problems is making tables. When making tables, students are required to put the problem data in an organized form. Tables help students see the data more clearly, recognize when data is missing, and fill in the missing data with logical information.

When teaching this strategy to your students, you should address several important points. Students need to understand how to develop a table, including which items to list on the table, how to record the data on the table, and even how to determine when enough information has been gathered and the table is complete. Students must acquire the skill of recognizing and extending patterns in order to complete tables accurately. Another important skill is the ability to select the correct answer from the many numbers that are recorded on the table. Spend time addressing each of these issues to ensure that students have a solid understanding of this strategy.

Constructing a Table

Tables show the relationship between two or more items. Take the following data, for example: **When shopping, each box of cereal**

costs $2.99. A table like the one below can help students find out the cost for 2, 3, 4, or 5 boxes of cereal. In this problem, there is a relationship between *cost* and *number of boxes*, and the table shows that relationship. Every box of cereal costs $2.99, so each time a box of cereal is added to the top row of the table, $2.99 must be added to the corresponding column on the bottom row.

number of boxes	1	2	3	4	5
cost	$2.99	$5.98	$8.97	$11.96	$14.95

A critical step in helping students create tables is to help them decide which two items have a *relationship*. Having a relationship means that one item is connected to the other in a predictable way. Model tables with several problems to help your students begin to see which items are related and therefore belong in the table.

Problem: **I can fit 5 people in one car. How many cars will I need for 20 people?**

There is a relationship between **number of people** and **number of cars,** so the table should show those two items. (*If I have 1 car, then I can fit 5 people in it. So, if I have 2 cars, then I can fit [5 + 5] or 10 people. If I* have 3 cars, I can fit [5 + 5 + 5] or 15 people, and so on.) The relationship always stays the same: for every 1 car, I can fit 5 people.

To help students develop this skill, you might ask them to read a problem and underline the two items that go together.

One balloon costs 25¢. How much do three balloons cost?

It takes 2 eggs to make 1 cake. How many eggs do I need to make 4 cakes?

Once students begin to recognize the two items that have a relationship, you can demonstrate how to create a table with those two items. Have students in pairs or groups practice setting up tables from a series of problems. Working with a partner or team will allow students to hear one another's ideas and will help them learn to recognize that when they see a relationship between items in a problem, it is a "table" problem.

Once students are able to recognize a table problem and set up the rows, labeled with each item name, it is time to help students extend the numbers across each row. Consider the balloon problem above. Initially, you will need to talk students through each step: "If I have 2 balloons, how much will it cost?" As students think through the problem—1 balloon costs 25¢, so 2 balloons must cost 25¢ + 25¢ or 50¢—the numbers can be recorded on the table. Do this on the blackboard or overhead projector to help students see the construction of the table as they talk through it.

number of balloons	1	2
cost	25¢	50¢

Recognizing and Extending Patterns

Although initially students will complete the numbers in each row by calculating 25¢ + 25¢ + 25¢ for the balloon problem, they will soon discover that they do not need to figure out each number if they recognize a pattern: *"Hey, these numbers go 25¢, 50¢, 75¢, the next number is going to be $1.00! It keeps adding 25¢!"* In this step, students will begin to rec-

ognize the role of patterns. As patterns emerge, students will extend them to continue the table. As I discussed in the previous chapter, patterns are very important in our number system. Point out the patterns as they appear in students' tables. Your students will begin to realize that finding a pattern, and being able to continue it, will help them solve problems.

Deciding When to Stop the Pattern

Students may need help in deciding when to end their table. When they are just learning to make tables, they continue the pattern to the end of the paper—and some students creatively go beyond that! There is a clue in each problem that will help students decide when their table is long enough. Let's look back at the balloon problem:

One balloon costs 25¢. How much do three balloons cost?

The first part of this problem tells us the relationship. The second part contains our clue as to where to stop our table. You could ask students the following questions to help them figure out when to stop the pattern.

What is the question we are asked to solve? (*How much do three balloons cost?*)

What do we know? (*We want 3 balloons.*)

What do we want to find out? (*How much it costs.*)

If we continue our table to three balloons, we will have our answer. Have students find and circle the clue that tells them when to stop their table.

One balloon costs 25¢. How much do three balloons cost?

Selecting the Correct Answer

The final stumbling block for students in solving problems by making tables comes after the table is created. Many students are quick to recognize the relationship and create the table but have a difficult time choosing the correct answer from the many numbers recorded on the table. This is a critical step, since the creation of the table alone does not solve the problem—it only provides the data from which to choose the answer. It is essential that teachers demonstrate how to locate the answer among all the values on the table.

First, ask students to go back to the question: **How much do three balloons cost?** Have them locate 3 balloons on their table and then look for the cost that corresponds to that number of balloons. It will be in the same column on the table, directly above or below the 3. Students might place their finger on the number three and then move their finger directly up or down on the chart to find the matching answer. Tell students that rereading the question will help them locate the right answer.

number of balloons	1	2	3
cost		25¢	50¢	75¢

I know this: It's part of the question!

This must be the answer!

Solving More Sophisticated Table Problems

In some cases, the answer to the problem does not appear on the table itself. Consider the following problem:

If you are purchasing cupcakes at $0.69 each, how many cupcakes can you buy for $3.00?

Although $3.00 will not appear on the table, viewing a completed table will help students decide what the answer is. When looking at a table like the one below, students will see that they will be able to afford 4 cupcakes, but do not have enough money for 5.

number of cupcakes	1	2	3	4	5
cost	$0.69	$1.38	$2.07	$2.76	$3.45

More sophisticated problems may require tables that have more than two items, like the following:

For the math activity, each student needed one ruler, three strips of paper, and four paper clips. How many rulers, strips of paper, and paper clips were needed for a group of six students?

There is a relationship between three items, which is represented by the table below.

number of rulers	1	2	3	4	5	6
number of strips of paper	3	6	9	12	15	18
number of paper clips	4	8	12	16	20	24

CLASSROOM-TESTED TIP

Locating the Answer on a Table

This step can be practiced in an easy, hands-on manner using transparent plastic chips. Refer to the balloon problem again. After your students create the table, give each one a chip. Begin to pose questions and ask students to place their chip on the answer from their table. "If I bought 2 balloons, how much would they cost?" "If I paid 75¢, how many balloons did I buy?" As students move their chips to indicate the answer, the teacher should walk around the room to assess students' understanding of this skill. An initial demonstration with transparent chips on an overhead projector will help prepare students for the independent practice and will reinforce the skill for students who are still developing in their understanding.

CLASSROOM-TESTED TIP

A Hands-On Introduction to Making Tables

Pose a problem:
Bear stickers cost 5¢ each. How much money will you need to buy 4 stickers?

Ask students:
"What are we trying to find out? What information in the problem will help us?"

Allow students to explore some ways to solve the problem using sticker and coin manipulatives. Ask students to share some of the ways they solved the problem. Begin to demonstrate a possible strategy by creating a table on the overhead projector with overhead coins and overhead bears.

As you fill in the table, ask students to tell you how many coins to place in each section of the table. Continue the table until you find the cost of 4 stickers. Ask students to use their stickers and coins to find the cost of 5 stickers, 6 stickers, 7 stickers, and so on.

Pose the questions:
"What if we didn't have coins and stickers to help us solve this problem? Is there a way we could use this strategy without the actual objects?"

Replace the objects with numbers to create a table like the one below. Have students compare the two tables to be sure the values are the same.

Number of stickers	1	2	3	4
Cost	5¢	10¢	15¢	20¢

Ask students:
"Is the answer the same? Do you notice anything about the numbers?"

Discuss the patterns that students see on the table. Ask students if knowing the pattern could help them solve the problem, and if so, how?

A Look at Student Work

It is helpful to present beginners with tables that are already constructed with numbers partially filled in. Students can then look at the tables to see the relationship and continue the patterns that have already been started for them (see Figure 6–1).

As students become more skilled at completing tables, you can give them less information and ask them to create more of the table on their own. To provide practice at a more sophisticated level, give students just the name labels for the table and ask them to find the initial values from the data in the problem and then continue the patterns to extend the table.

When students become adept at finding initial values, it is time to present them with blank tables and ask them to decide on both the items and the initial values. Providing them with a blank table will focus them on the strategy they are working with and get them jump-started.

With practice, students will become proficient at creating tables. Then you will want to assist them in developing the reasoning

Buying Peanut Butter*

You can buy 2 jars of peanut butter for 3 dollars. How much will it cost to buy 6 jars of peanut butter? Finish the table to help you figure out the answer.

jars of peanut butter	2	4	6	8	10
dollars		3	6	9	12	15

Circle the answer on your table.

Do you see any patterns on your table? Describe one pattern.

Jars of Peanutbutter you count by twos.

FIGURE 6–1   This student only needed to extend the patterns on the table. *Skippy © is a registered trademark of Bestfoods. Used with permission.

Tropical Bananas

Bananas are sold by the pound. Use the data on the grocery ad to decide how much it will cost to buy 12 pounds of bananas. Use a table to help you figure out the cost.

cost	79¢	$1.58	$2.37	$3.16	$3.95	$4.74	$5.53
pounds	2	4	6	8	10	12	14

Explain why using a table is a good strategy for solving this problem.

This problem is asking you to find out how much 12 pounds of bananas will cost. In order to do that, I need to gather my information I already know. I know it costs 79¢ for two pounds of bananas. That is the relationship in this problem.

To get the solution I used the method of making a table. One row I labeled cost and the other row I labeled pounds.

In the row cost I increased it to the equivalent cost for 12 lbs. of bananas by increments of 79¢. In the column labeled pounds I increased by increments of 2 to 12. As I completed the table, I noticed I could have solved the problem by multiplying 79¢ times 6. I prefer using a table though because it shows the information I need and other information visually. The relationship is the most important part of the problem. If I did not know it, I could not make a table. After completing the table, I know that the solution to this problem is for 12 pounds of tropical bananas it costs $4.74.

FIGURE 6–2   This student's writing reflects an in-depth understanding of this problem-solving strategy.

skill of deciding when this strategy should be used. At this point, it is best to stop providing the table for the students and allow them to make the choice of an appropriate strategy. Asking students to justify their choice of strategies will help you see if they've truly mastered not only the mechanics of the skill, but the concept of when it is best used.

In analyzing students' writing, we can see the development of their thinking from a very basic level to a very sophisticated understanding. Look at the work sample in Figure 6–2, for example. After repeated practice and solid classroom instruction, this sixth grader is able to eloquently explain how to set up tables and how the table helped her solve the problem.

Reflecting on the Strategy

Asking students to write about and talk about their tables is a great way to assess students' understanding of this strategy. Try prompts like these:

▌ Explain how making a table helped you find the answer.

■ Explain how you know which number on the table is the answer to the problem.

■ Explain how you know which two items in the problem should be used to create your table.

■ Describe the patterns you see on your table.

■ Explain how you knew when you had enough data on your table to solve the problem.

■ Why was making a table a good strategy for solving this problem?

CHAPTER SEVEN

Strategy: Make an Organized List

Through group and classroom discussions, students can examine a

variety of approaches and learn to evaluate appropriate strategies for a

given solution.   NCTM

Making an organized list is a valuable strategy when students are faced with problems that require determining all the possible combinations for a given situation. Students might be exploring all the possible double-dip ice cream cone combinations that can be made using vanilla, chocolate, and strawberry ice cream or the number of possible drink/snack combinations that can be made from milk, cola, cookies, and peanuts. Students who are able to organize data into lists are able to systematically figure out the correct number of possibilities.

Organization Is the Key

The most important point to emphasize when teaching this strategy is that students should make an *organized* list. In figuring out all the

---

CLASSROOM-TESTED TIP

Demonstrating the Need for Organization

Try a demonstration with three students in your class. Ask them to get in a line to sharpen their pencils. Create the line in front of the class, for example, Katie, then Joe, then Erica. Ask the class how many other ways they might line up. As students in the class suggest other ways in which to order the three students, switch their order in the line. After a while, ask students "Is that all the possible ways? How many ways were there? Are you sure we've tried them all? Are you sure we haven't repeated any?" Ask students to talk with a partner and see if they can figure out a way to be sure that you have all the possible orders and haven't repeated any. You might prompt them with questions such as "How many ways can they line up if Katie is first? If Joe is first? If Erica is first?" Students may come up with the idea of writing down each possibility, or they may even come up with an organized method to be sure they don't miss any possibilities. Praise their logical thinking as they share their ideas. Begin again, this time keeping an organized list.

---

possible combinations, students often randomly list the possibilities. As students list combinations in a random fashion, they become confused and unsure of which combinations have already been given. Teach students to begin with one item and then exhaust all possible combinations with that item before moving on to another item to help them proceed in an organized manner and recognize when they have listed all of the possibilities.

Working from Concrete to Abstract

Hands-on introductory activities help students visualize this strategy. You may begin with actual objects, move to drawings of objects, and then move to lists or tree diagrams. Provide students with opportunities to play with the combinations in a concrete form. While they try the different combinations, encourage an organized way of proceeding and model how to record the combinations that have been tried. Once concepts have been established, remember to move students from a concrete to an abstract (paper and pencil) method for representing the problem. As students strengthen their understanding of the concept, we want to wean them from the manipulatives and show them how to create lists and tree diagrams to represent the different combinations.

Laying the Foundation for More Sophisticated Skills

As students work on organized lists, they develop the groundwork for more sophisticated mathematical skills. Students may begin to notice patterns in their answers and may even discover mathematical formulas that help them arrive at their answers without making lists.

In some problems, the order is a critical element in determining the number of combinations. Consider for example the problem in which students are asked to find the number of possible three-digit numbers that could be created using the digits 1, 2, and 3. The number 123 is different from 132, which is different

---

CLASSROOM-TESTED TIP

Introducing Organized Lists

Give students a worksheet with three cups and two circles as shown in Appendix G. Ask them to color the cups red, yellow, and orange to represent fruit punch, lemonade, and orange drink. Ask them to color the circles brown and yellow to represent chocolate and sugar cookies. Have students cut out the cups and cookies. Ask the students how many drink/cookie combinations are possible. Allow them to experiment with the paper drinks and cookies. After they've experimented, ask some students to share their answers. (There will probably be a variety of answers!) Tell students you are going to explore the problem together. Be sure to record each combination as you demonstrate it for the class. Show students how to begin with one item, such as fruit punch, and determine all the combinations for that item before moving on.

Fruit punch and chocolate cookie
Fruit punch and sugar cookie

Ask students, "Are there any other combinations that you can make with fruit punch?" Students should be able to tell you without a doubt that there are no more, since you've used both kinds of cookies. Move on to lemonade and follow the same process. When you are finished, ask students if they are sure you named all of the possibilities. They should feel confident that no combination has been missed. When having students make lists to solve problems, try to give purpose to the activity by asking students to indicate their preference. Asking "Which drink/cookie combination would you choose?" will provide a reason for having to figure out all of those possibilities.

from 231. Each ordered group is a different possibility. As students work on similar permutation problems, they develop skills in factorials. They may find that three digits can be arranged in 3! ways or $3 \times 2 \times 1$ ways or 6 ways.

Consider the problem in which students need to determine the number of shirt/short combinations possible with 2 shirts (blue and green) and 3 shorts (red, yellow, and black). It doesn't matter whether the student records a blue shirt with red shorts or red shorts with a blue shirt; regardless of the order in which they are recorded, they are the same clothing combination. As students work on similar combination problems, they often notice a formula—if there are x of one item and y of another item, then there are xy possibilities. Students will discover that 2 shirts and 3 shorts will yield 2×3 or 6 possible combinations.

While younger students will rely on lists to solve the problems, older students may begin to use the mathematical formulas to find their answers. When first experimenting with formulas, students may continue to use lists to verify their answers and test to be sure that the formulas will yield the correct results.

A Look at Student Work

Initially, students can experiment with actual objects or manipulatives. Once the concept of combinations has been presented in a concrete way, students may begin to draw objects rather than use the actual items (see Figure 7–1).

Students will soon see that a list will give them the same information as the drawings and is much easier and quicker to use. (If they don't see this, guide them to this understanding!) Students may begin by listing the entire word, but they will soon see that initials or abbreviations work well and save time (see Figure 7–2).

Making Valentines

Imagine that you decided to make valentines for your friends. You can cut the paper into three shapes - round, square, or heart-shaped. You can decorate them with stripes or polka dots. How many different kinds of valentines can you make? Show how you solved the problem.

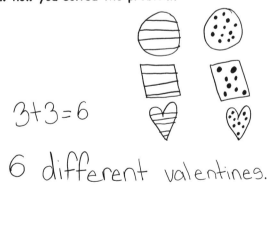

$3 + 3 = 6$

6 different valentines.

FIGURE 7–1   This student draws each possible valentine.

Lunch Choices

Jennifer wants to order a sandwich and a drink. Look at the menu below to decide how many different choices she has.

LUNCH MENU

<u>SANDWICHES</u>
Chicken
Ham
Tuna

<u>DRINKS</u>
Lemonade
Milk

CL
CM
HL
HM
TL
TM

There are 6 diffrent ways.

How did making an organized list help you solve this problem?

Making a organized list helped me solved this problem by helping me keep things in order and helping me by not writing something twice.

FIGURE 7–2   This student decides to use initials for each sandwich and drink.

Tree diagrams are another effective way to represent combinations. Although these are technically diagrams rather than lists, they are introduced at this time because of their ability to assist with combination problems. It is important to demonstrate for students how to create these diagrams to represent the data and how to count the final column to get the total number of possible combinations (see Figure 7–3).

Remind students that a list or tree diagram is not the answer to a problem, it is a strategy to help them arrive at the answer. The problem may be asking how many combinations are possible or which combination the student would choose. The lists and diagrams are tools to help students find the answer.

Reflecting on the Strategy

Don't forget to have students write about and talk about their strategy for solving the problem. Try prompts like these:

■ How did making a list help you solve this problem?
■ Why is it important to record your combinations?
■ Explain why it's important to be organized when making your list.
■ Why was making a list a good strategy for solving this problem?

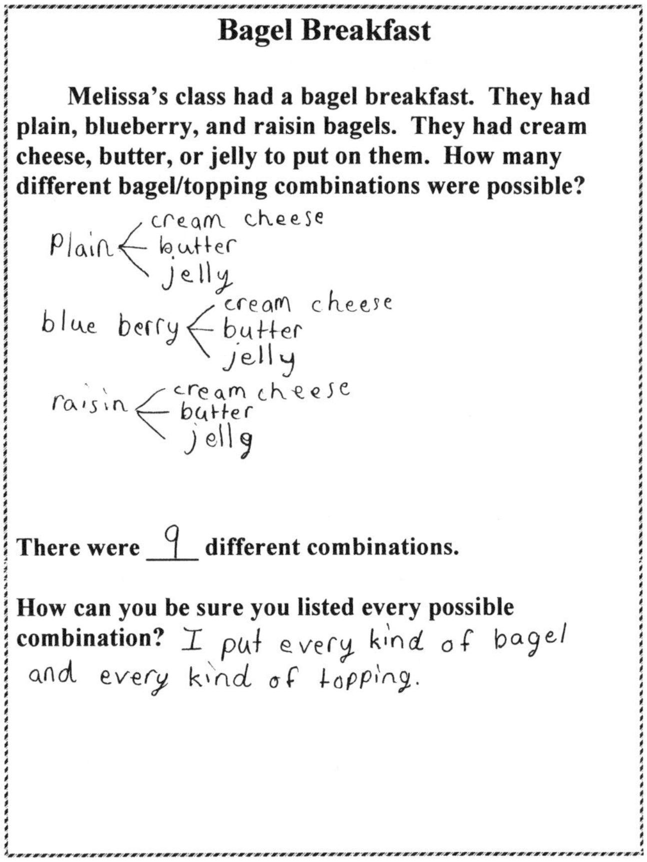

Bagel Breakfast

Melissa's class had a bagel breakfast. They had plain, blueberry, and raisin bagels. They had cream cheese, butter, or jelly to put on them. How many different bagel/topping combinations were possible?

There were __9__ different combinations.

How can you be sure you listed every possible combination? I put every kind of bagel and every kind of topping.

FIGURE 7–3 In this tree diagram, the student correctly counts 9 combinations.

■ Are you sure there are no other possible combinations? Why?
■ Is there a way to solve this problem other than making a list? Explain.

CHAPTER EIGHT

Strategy: Draw a Picture or Diagram

The act of representing encourages children to focus on the essential characteristics of a situation. NCTM

The old adage, "A picture is worth a thousand words," can be true in problem-solving. Constructing a picture or diagram helps students visualize the problem. After reading a problem, students should be able to use the data to create a picture or diagram that represents the problem. Problems that initially appear complex often become easy to solve when students are able to draw or diagram them.

Consider the following problem:

Colleen is shorter than Brendan. Michael is taller than Brendan but shorter than Kevin. Who is the tallest?

This type of problem often generates immediate anxiety because of the confusing wording; however, if you teach students how to draw a picture or diagram to represent each piece of information, you will show that it's a simple problem (see Figure 8–1). A diagram serves to clarify the situation. Students can draw simple pictures, following each clue. Their drawings will reveal the answer.

Another way to diagram the same problem might be to simply write each person's name in order, top to bottom or tallest to shortest, following the clues in the problem.

Colleen   Michael   Brendan   Kevin

FIGURE 8–1　Students' simple drawings show them how easy it can be to find a solution.

First fact:
Colleen is shorter than Brendan.

Brendan
Colleen

The fact is represented by Colleen's name being written below (indicating shorter than) Brendan's name in the simple diagram.

Second fact:
Michael is taller than Brendan.

Michael
Brendan
Colleen

If Michael is taller than Brendan, his name goes on top of Brendan's in the diagram.

Third fact:
Michael is shorter than Kevin.

Kevin
Michael
Brendan
Colleen

If Michael is shorter than Kevin, then Kevin's name must be on top of his in the diagram. Now the diagram is complete and not only is it clear who is tallest, but we know the exact order of heights from tallest to shortest. (*Tip:* When teaching this strategy, remind students to leave spaces between items as they work on the solution. That way, they will be able to insert information at any place in their diagram.)

A New Meaning for the Word Picture

In problem solving, pictures should not be works of art. Discourage students from adding unnecessary details to their pictures. Coloring the picture is unnecessary unless the colors represent some of the data. Students need to be reminded that a square can represent a house or a car—the picture does not need to be realistic. Students often spend so much time creating a detailed picture that they never end up solving the problem. Focus students on the problem-solving process.

CLASSROOM-TESTED TIP

Introducing Pictures/Diagrams to Solve Problems

Pose the following problem to students: **There were 8 children at a party. Each child could choose the flavor of sherbet he or she wanted for a snack. Half of the children chose orange sherbet. Half of those who were left chose lime. The others had raspberry. How many children had each kind of sherbet?**

Ask students for the answers to the problem. Students will probably be confused by the problem initially. Ask them if seeing a picture of the problem might help them find the answer. Have them draw a picture to represent the eight children, but rather than drawing children, ask them just to draw eight circles—one for each child at the party. Demonstrate for them on the chalkboard or overhead pro-jector. Read the first part of the problem together and ask the students to color half of the circles orange to represent the children who ate orange sherbet. Ask them how many children still need to pick a flavor (4). Read the next part of the problem and ask them to color half of the circles that are left green to represent the children who had lime sherbet. Ask the students how many children still need to pick a flavor (2). Read the last part of the problem. Ask the students to color the remaining circles red to represent raspberry sherbet. Reread the problem. Ask the students how many children ate each kind of sherbet, this time having them use their drawing to help them. Students should be easily able to count the number of children who had each flavor. Ask students to talk about what was easy or hard about the problem and how the diagram helped them solve it.

A Look at Student Work

For very young students, drawing pictures is an aid in helping them understand the simplest math concepts. As students learn to add 2 + 3, they draw pictures of two objects and three objects. This enables them to count their pictures to find the total. The picture helps to make the problem real and understandable. As students grow older and their ability to work in the abstract increases, they no longer rely on pictures for many math concepts. There will, however, always be some problems that become more clear when a picture or diagram is used (see Figure 8–2).

Students are often quick to answer problems before fully investigating the data. A picture can serve to demonstrate the error in their judgment. In the problem in Figure 8–3,

Splitting a Sub

Jean bought a very big submarine sandwich to share with her friends for lunch. She cut it into four pieces so that everyone could have some. How many cuts did she have to make?

3 cuts

How many cuts did she make?

I solved this problem by

drawing a picture. I thot you needed 4 cuts but you only need 3.

FIGURE 8–3 This student began to draw "cuts" in her diagram expecting to draw 4 "cuts." Her drawing helped her recognize the error in her initial thinking.

The Bags of Candy

Haley has 4 bags of candy. There are 3 jellybeans and 1 peppermint in each bag. How many jellybeans does Haley have? 12

How many peppermints does Haley have? 4

(Will a picture or diagram help?)

Explain how drawing a picture helped you solve this problem. Drawing a picture helps you because you can see it on your paper and count it easily.

FIGURE 8–2 This student's simple diagram helped her find a solution.

Emily's Party

Emily had a party. She invited two guests. Her guests each invited two guests and those two guests each invited three guests. How many people were at Emily's party?

Explain the strategy you used to solve the problem.
There were 19 people at Emily's party. 18 people were invited as guests. I got my answer by drawing a picture of Emily's guests and all the people they invited. Drawing a picture helps me answer the problem by showing me visually how many people were at the party.

FIGURE 8–4 This upper-elementary student was able to diagram a more complex problem.

4 is often a student's first answer, until a picture helps the student see the problem more clearly.

As students become more sophisticated, they find that diagrams are useful ways to illustrate problems for which solutions are not readily evident (see Figure 8–4).

Reflecting on the Strategy

Don't forget to have students write and talk about their strategies. It is by communicating about what they've done that students solidify their understanding. In addition, the writing or discussion is a great way for teachers to get a glimpse of students' thinking. Try prompts like these:

- Why was drawing a picture a good strategy for solving this problem?
- Does a picture need to be detailed to help you solve a problem? Explain.
- Explain how your diagram helped you solve this problem.

CHAPTER NINE

Strategy: Guess, Check, and Revise

When problem solving becomes an integral part of classroom

instruction and children experience success in solving problems, they

gain confidence in doing mathematics and develop persevering and

inquiring minds. NCTM

The Guess, Check, and Revise strategy is exactly what it sounds like—if you're not sure where to begin, take a guess! The guess, however, should be reasonable and is only the beginning of the process. After plugging the guess into the problem situation, a student will need to adjust the guess until the correct answer is found. In the words of a third grader: *"You guess and then you check. If it's too high, use lower numbers. If it's too low then use higher numbers."* That sounds easy enough!

Beginning with a Guess

Often students are faced with a problem and they don't know how to begin. While a guess may be a good way to begin tackling the problem, the guess should be a reasonable one. Students should be able to use their estimation skills to get "in the ballpark." Discuss initial guesses with students. Together, look for clues in the problem that will help them make educated guesses and in so doing, lessen

the number of revisions they will have to make. If a problem asks for three consecutive numbers that equal 33, students should not be starting with a guess of 28. It would not be reasonable to think that 28, 29, and 30 would add up to 33. If you notice unreasonable student guesses, practice just the first step of this problem-solving strategy. Pose problems to your students and ask them to estimate (guess) the answer. Have students discuss the reasonableness of their guesses with a partner or team. Ask them to share their ideas on how they came up with their guesses. Logical reasoning and number sense play an important role in this strategy.

Revising the Guess

Revision is the critical part of this strategy. It is unlikely that students will guess the correct answer on the first try, so they must then plug their guesses into the problem and adjust the initial guess until they've found the correct answer. Students will need to recognize when their guess is too large or too small and will need to be able to make adjustments until the answer is found.

Thinking aloud is especially important when demonstrating this strategy. Both in selecting a first guess and in revising guesses throughout the process, it is important that students understand the thinking involved in each step. Students need to hear your thought processes as you adjust and readjust your answers. Students need to know it's okay not to get the answer on the first guess. After modeling a few problems for the class, you might want to ask students to work with a partner to hear each other's thinking during the revision stage.

Using Guess, Check, and Revise with Equations

A student might look at the equation below and not know where to begin. This is when students often put their heads down or choose not to go on because they don't know how to get started. The Guess, Check, and Revise strategy will provide them with both a starting point and a method to figure out the answer.

$$\underline{\hspace{2cm}} \times 2 + 10 = 26$$

Encourage them to try a number in the blank, for example, 4.

$4 \times 2 + 10 = 26$??? Actually, $4 \times 2 + 10 = 18$ *"This answer is too small, so let's try a larger number. How about 6?"*

$6 \times 2 + 10 = 22$ *"Closer, but still too small. How about 8?"*

$8 \times 2 + 10 = 26$ *"It worked! 8 is the correct answer."*

Without knowing how to begin, the student was able to find the correct answer by using the Guess, Check, and Revise method.

Understanding the Role of Positive Attitudes

This strategy depends on the development of positive problem-solving attitudes as discussed in Chapter One. Students must be risk takers and jump in, even when they are unsure how to begin. Students are sometimes hesitant to guess an answer. Assure them that it is a fine way to begin a problem—as long as they check their guess and adjust it as needed. Students must also be patient and persistent as they check and revise each guess. Each guess should bring them closer to the correct answer.

A Look at Student Work

As you can see from the number sentences on the side of the student's paper in Figure 9–1, the child made several attempts before he found a workable solution. It is evident from his trials that he did a good job adjusting his work. When he guessed too low at first, he chose larger numbers on his second try. When those numbers were too large, he adjusted them down and found a correct answer.

Now, look at Figure 9–2. This student shows solid reasoning in his revision. In addition, his comments show that he recognized and eliminated an unreasonable response (cereal).

Consider the student work in Figure 9–3. This sixth-grade student needed to employ a

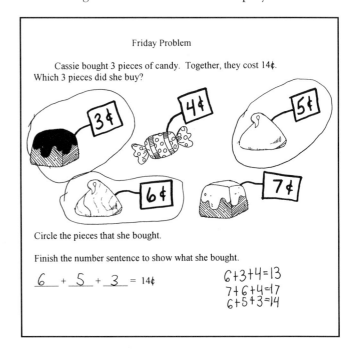

FIGURE 9–1 A look at this student's guesses shows thoughtful revisions that lead to a correct answer.

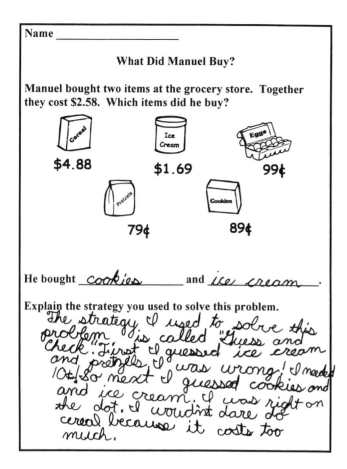

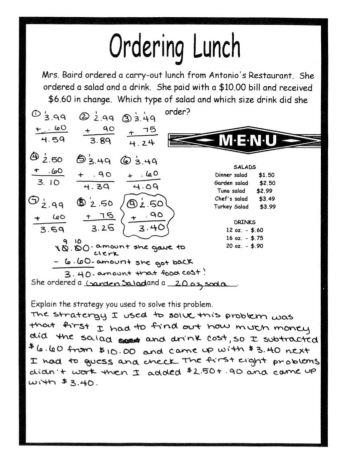

FIGURE 9–2 This student's writing shows that his first guess was a thoughtful one as he eliminated cereal as a possible item before beginning his search for the solution.

FIGURE 9–3 This student does not keep the target cost ($3.40) in mind as she searches for a solution. Her initial guess includes an item costing $3.99 From trial 1 to trial 2 she appears to be getting closer to the answer, then in trial 3 she again includes an item costing $3.49, which is more than the target cost. An analysis of her trials shows that she is not making thoughtful revisions.

CLASSROOM-TESTED TIP

Introducing Guess, Check, and Revise

Cut out ads for five different items from a grocery store advertisement, for example, pretzels $1.29, cookies $2.50, chocolate cake $3.83, pizza $4.75, and watermelon $5.45. For younger students, just use pictures of five food items and give each item a rounded price such as pretzels $1.00, cookies $2.00, chocolate cake $3.00, pizza $4.00, watermelon $5.00. Tell the students that they are being sent to the store to buy two items. The total cost of the items is _____. They will need to figure out which two items you want them to buy. Have a student guess two items. Together, figure out the cost of the items. Ask the students to tell you if these two items cost too much, too little, or just the right amount. If the guess was not correct, tell the students that they will need to try again. Ask for another guess. Check the guess and again ask students, "Is the guess too high, too low, or just right?" Students may be asked to respond with thumbs up (too high), thumbs down (too low), or a flat hand parallel to the ground (just right). Praise students who use this information in their next guess. Continue until you've found an answer. Try a few more, with students working in pairs or groups to allow them to discuss their guesses and revisions. Praise students for reasonable guesses and logical revisions.

two-step process to solve the problem. Although her description is clear and accurate, her calculations show that her revisions were not well thought-out but appear to be random guesses. Asking students to number their trials will help you assess whether their revisions were thoughtful ones.

Building the Foundation for More Advanced Skills

Problems that are solved in middle school and high school with algebraic equations can be solved by elementary students using the Guess, Check, and Revise strategy. Consider the following problem, for example:

Lisa opened her book and saw the two consecutive page numbers. The sum of the page numbers was 43. What are the numbers?

In algebra, you write an equation: $x + (x + 1) = 43$.

In Guess, Check, and Revise, you try a page number, say 20. The next page would then be 21. The sum would be 41. That's too low. Time to revise! Try page numbers 21 and 22. The sum would be 43. The Guess, Check, and Revise strategy is another way to solve the same problem.

Reflecting on the Strategy

Don't forget to have students write about and talk about the strategy. Try prompts like these:

▍ How did Guess, Check, and Revise help you solve this problem?
▍ Explain why revising is so important.
▍ Why did you choose this strategy to help you solve the problem?
▍ Why is it important to be persistent when solving problems?

CHAPTER TEN

Strategy: Use Logical Reasoning

Reasoning is fundamental to the knowing and doing of mathematics.

NCTM

L ogical reasoning is an important skill for solving problems. Many of the other strategies I have discussed depend on logical reasoning. Students need to use logical reasoning when adjusting their guesses in Guess, Check, and Revise and analyzing their pictures or diagrams. In many cases, it is hard to separate logical reasoning from other strategies. Some problems, however, utilize logical reasoning as the primary problem-solving strategy. Whether it is the primary strategy or is

---

CLASSROOM-TESTED TIP

Introducing Logical Reasoning

To introduce the concept of logical reasoning to students, start with some hands-on activities. Ask students to manipulate objects based on a series of clues. One activity would be to give each student four shapes: a circle, a triangle, a rectangle, and a square (see Appendix G). Present the following clues and ask the students to put the shapes in a row from left to right on their desks based on the clues.

■ The first figure is a 3-sided figure.
■ The figure with four equal sides is second.
■ The circle is not last.

Ask the students to share the order of their shapes with a partner. Ask them to discuss any differences and decide which order fits the clues. Walk around the room to visually monitor their progress. Have one pair of students explain why they placed the shapes in the order that they did. Point out to students that some information is stated (*The figure with four equal sides is second.*) while other information must be inferred, or figured out. If the circle is not last, where must it be? If the first figure is a three-sided figure, which figure is first? Remind students that using logical reasoning involves thinking about information and making some judgments based on what is known. Order the shapes in a different way, using different clues. You may even ask students to write their own clues and share them with their partner to see if their partner can order the shapes. Try similar activities, ordering different colors or familiar objects such as pencil, crayon, eraser, paper clip.

combined with other problem-solving strategies, logical thinking is of critical importance to students' problem-solving success.

In this strategy, students need to practice analyzing clues or bits of information presented in the problem and then use that information to help solve the problem. Techniques like process of elimination help students narrow down the possible solutions so they can arrive at a logical answer. Graphic organizers like matrices and Venn diagrams also help students organize data so they are able to draw appropriate conclusions.

Using a Logic Matrix

A matrix is one tool for keeping track of information and working through the process of piecing clues together. A matrix is a grid in which students record data. Consider the following problem:

Kathy, Lisa, and Dan each have a snack. One has a banana, one has a chocolate bar, and one has raisins. Dan does not like candy. Kathy peels her snack. Lisa's snack melts on a hot day. Which snack does each child have?

Students create a grid like the one in Figure 10–1. They fill in the grid with three names (Kathy, Lisa, Dan) and three possible snacks (banana, chocolate bar, and raisins). They then use the clues to work toward a solution.

Dan does not like candy. (*Then he must not be having a chocolate bar—I can put an x by chocolate on the grid.*)

	Banana	Chocolate bar	Raisins
Kathy	yes	x	x
Lisa	x	yes	x
Dan	x	x	yes

FIGURE 10–1   Information is organized on a matrix.

Kathy peels her snack. (*She must be having a banana. I can put a yes or check mark by banana. That also means I can put an x by chocolate and raisins for Kathy, since she only had one snack. And I can put an x by banana for Lisa and Dan, since they must have had the other snacks.*) Eliminating wrong answers will help students narrow down the possibilities.

Lisa's snack melts on a hot day. (*It must be chocolate! I can put an x by raisins for Lisa since I now know she had chocolate.*)

So, Dan must be having raisins for his snack!

Each clue brings students closer to a solution. The matrix helps them keep track of the clues.

When showing students how to use a matrix, remind them to read and think about each clue and to revisit clues a second time if the problem remains unsolved after one reading of the problem. Often, a clue has more meaning after another clue has been considered. Remind students that when they find an answer, they should eliminate the other boxes in the same row and column. There can only be one *yes* in each row and column.

Using a List to Organize Clues

A matrix is not the only way to sketch out a logic problem. Students can create lists on which they cross off items that are eliminated as possible answers.

Figuring out what is *not* the answer can be an important step in finally determining an answer. Students can keep track of clues by creating lists on which they cross off possibilities as they eliminate them. Consider the following problem:

Brendan plays basketball. The players on his team have the numbers 1–10 on their uniforms. Use the clues to help you decide Brendan's number.

> **His number is not an even number.**
> **His number is greater than 5.**
> **His number is a multiple of 3.**

Students can keep track of their progress toward a solution by making a list of numbers and then crossing off the unnecessary numbers as they analyze each clue.

His number is not an even number. (*I can cross off all the even numbers.*)

1 2̸ 3 4̸ 5 6̸ 7 8̸ 9 1̸0̸

His number is greater than 5. (*That means it isn't 1, 3, or 5.*)

1̸ 2̸ 3̸ 4̸ 5̸ 6̸ 7 8̸ 9 1̸0̸

His number is a multiple of 3. (*The only numbers left are 7 and 9, and 7 isn't a multiple of 3. The answer must be 9!*)

1̸ 2̸ 3̸ 4̸ 5̸ 6̸ 7̸ 8̸ ⑨ 1̸0̸

Using a Venn Diagram to Organize Ideas

Venn diagrams are also helpful tools in sorting out logic problems. Consider this problem:

The coach brought the ten players on Brendan's basketball team to the ice cream parlor to celebrate their big win. The players could order an ice cream cone, a soft drink, or both. Seven players had ice cream and six players had a soft drink. How many players had both?

Students can use a Venn diagram to organize the data for this problem. One side of the diagram should be labeled "ice cream cones" and the other side should be labeled "soft drinks." Each child should have ten manipulatives (color chips, toothpicks, pennies) to represent the ten basketball players. As students

begin to represent the data on the Venn diagram, they will first place seven chips in the ice cream cone circle. As students try to place six chips in the soft drink section of the diagram, they find that they do not have enough chips. Students can be challenged to experiment with placing their chips on the diagram until they find a placement that fits the data in the problem. Working in pairs will provide students with opportunities to talk about the location and reason for their placement choices. As students see that they can slide some chips into the center of the Venn diagram, they are able to solve the problem (see Figure 10–2.)

Model your thoughts by speaking aloud as you solve problems for your students. Thinking is an abstract process, but through think-alouds and graphic organizers, you can help your students "see" logical thinking.

A Look at Student Work

Study the student sample in Figure 10–3. This student used a list of numbers to help organize his clues. As he eliminated possible answers, he crossed them off his list.

Now consider the work in Figure 10–4. A Venn diagram became a helpful tool for this student, who was able to see the answer clearly after diagramming the problem.

The student whose work is shown in Figure 10–5 tackled a more complicated logic problem using a matrix. His explanation indicates his recognition that the matrix itself yields clues to solving the problem. He found an answer by noticing that there was only one box without an X in it.

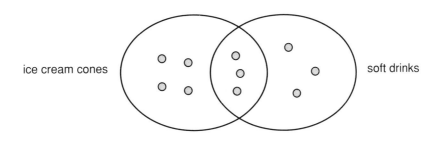

FIGURE 10–2 Using a Venn diagram allows students to visualize the problem.

How Old is Kim?

Use the clues to help you figure out how old Kim is.

1. She is less than 10 years old.
2. She is more than 7 years old.
3. She is not 8 years old.

How old is Kim?

X̶2̶ X̶3̶ X̶4̶ X̶5̶ 6 X̶7̶ X̶8̶ ⑨ X̶10̶ X̶11̶ X̶12̶

FIGURE 10–3   Following the clues and eliminating numbers by crossing them out helped lead this student to a solution.

Valentine Helpers

Miss Blackwood had 14 students help during the Valentine Party. Nine students passed out valentine cards. Eight students helped with refreshments. How many student helpers did both? Explain how you got your answer.

Three people did both. I got my answer by drawing a picture. First, I draw 14 student. Next, I circled 9 students then 8. Then I saw that 3 people did both because 3 students were overlapped.

FIGURE 10–4   This student used a Venn diagram to display problem data.

Library Days

At Glenn Dale Elementary School, Mrs. McConn, Mrs. Little, Mrs. Mack, Mr. Flin, and Miss Black all bring their classes to the school library on a different day of the week. Use the clues below to figure out which day each class goes to the library.

1. Either Miss Black's class or Mrs. McConn's class goes to the library on Wednesdays. The other class goes on Thursdays.
2. Mr. Flin's class goes to the library on a day whose name begins with the letter "T".
3. Mrs. Mack's class goes to the library two days before Miss Black's class.

	Mrs. McConn	Mrs. Little	Mrs. Mack	Mr. Flin	Miss Black
Monday	X	X	☺	X	X
Tuesday	X	X	X	☺	X
Wednesday	X	X	X	X	☺
Thursday	☺	X	X	X	X
Friday	X	☺	X	X	X

Explain how you were able to figure out which day Mrs. Little's class goes to the library. First I knew Mrs. McConn and Miss Black didn't go to the library on Mon., Tues., or Friday. Mr. Flin's class could only go on Tues. or Thursday because they start with a T. Miss Mack couldn't go on Wed., Thurs., or Friday because it's not 2 days before Miss Black's class, so Miss Little must go on Friday cause no one else does. It was the only one without an X.

Reflecting on the Strategy

Don't forget to have students write about and talk about how they solved the problems. Try prompts like these:

- Explain the strategy you used to solve this problem.
- Explain why you set up your matrix or Venn diagram the way you did.
- Explain how the matrix or Venn diagram helped you solve the problem.
- How did eliminating some possibilities help you solve the problem?

FIGURE 10–5   As this student read clues and recorded data on a matrix, he began to see the data more clearly.

CHAPTER ELEVEN

Strategy: Work Backward

Exploring, investigating, describing, and explaining mathematical ideas promote communication. Teachers facilitate this process when they pose probing questions and invite children to explain their thinking.

NCTM

We use the Work Backward strategy when we know how a situation ends, but we don't know how it started. The strategy works well for problems such as the following: **If it's 3:00 P.M. and we just spent 15 minutes correcting papers, what time did we start correcting papers?** or, **If I have $4.00 in my pocket after going to the grocery store, and I spent $2.50 at the store, how much money did I have in my pocket to start?** Simple one-step problems are a good way to introduce this strategy to students. Students learn to reverse their thinking—to begin with what they know about how the situation ended in order to figure out what happened at the start.

Consider the following sample problem:

Mrs. Higgins went to Burger Barn. She spent half of the money she had on lunch. Then, she spent 75¢ on dessert. She had $1.00 left. How much money did she have at the start?

In working through the problem, students will need to begin with what they know and reverse the actions to find out how the situation began.

"We know she has $1.00 now. The last thing she did was spend 75¢ on dessert, so I'll add the 75¢ to the $1.00 she has and find that she had $1.75 before she bought dessert. If she spent half of what she had on lunch and was left with $1.75, she must have spent $1.75 on lunch. $1.75 + $1.75 = $3.50. She must have had $3.50 at the start.

A critical step in ensuring student success with this strategy is reminding students to routinely check the answer. Because students often become confused when reversing operations, a simple check will allow them to find any mistakes.

"Let's see if that works. If Mrs. Higgins had $3.50 and spent half of it on lunch, she would have had $1.75 left. If she then spent 75¢ on

CLASSROOM-TESTED TIP

Introducing Working Backward

Give each student a small bag of candy or plastic chips that represent candy and a copy of the bag pattern shown in Appendix G. Tell the students that you are going to read them a problem. In this problem, they will know about what happens at the end of the story, but they won't know how it started. Their job is to figure out how the story began. Just like a detective, they will be using clues to re-create what happened in the story.

Pose the following problem to students:

Kathy had a bag of candy. She gave 3 pieces to her sister. Then, she gave 5 pieces to her mother. She had 4 pieces of candy left. How many did she have to start?

Ask the students to tell you how many pieces Kathy has now (4). Have each student put four pieces of candy (or chips) in the candy bag (or by placing their chips on the bag cutout). Ask the students what happened right before Kathy was left with four pieces of candy. (*She gave 5 pieces to her mother.*) Ask them to imagine that she had not done that. Each student should take five pieces of candy and put them back into the bag, as if Kathy

had not given them to her mother. Ask students how many pieces of candy are in the bag now (9). Then, ask the students what Kathy did right before she gave candy to her mother. (*She gave 3 pieces to her sister.*) Ask them to pretend she had not given candy to her sister and put the three pieces back into the bag. Ask the students how many pieces are in the bag now (12). Ask students if Kathy gave candy to anyone else (they should say "no"). Have students count how many pieces of candy were in Kathy's bag to start (12).

Ask students to check their answer by acting out the problem with the twelve pieces of candy. As you read the story to the students, have them remove the candy from the bag as it is given away. Do the students end with 4 pieces of candy just like Kathy? If so, their answer must be correct.

Give an initial demonstration on an overhead projector to help students visualize the problem before they join in the activity. Try the activity several times, changing the quantities of candy given away. For older students, begin with larger numbers or use fractions such as as $\frac{1}{2}$ or $\frac{1}{4}$.

dessert, she would have $1.00 left. That matches the data in the problem! I was right!"

Working Backward with Equations

Another way to demonstrate working backward is to use simple addition and subtraction equations.

$$\text{_____} + 3 - 1 = 12$$

Have students begin at the end of the equation. Ask them to think about what was done and work backward reversing the operations, to solve the problem.

"I have 12 now. The last thing I did was subtract one, so I'll add one. After that I can subtract 3, since I added 3 in the equation. What I have now should be the number I started with."

Remember, a very important step in the Work Backward strategy is checking the answer by plugging it back into the problem and seeing if it works. Remind students to always do this.

$$\underline{10} + 3 - 1 = 12 \qquad \textit{It works!}$$

A Look at Student Work

When beginning this strategy with students, give them one-step problems to help them get a feel for the process. In the sample in Figure 11–1, the student first used coins to re-create the problem and then moved to the abstract thinking shown in the sample.

As students become more sophisticated with the process, give them problems with two or three steps. Students become adept at

Working Backwards

Carlos spent 20¢ on a postcard. He has 53¢ left in his piggy bank. How much did he have to start?

$$\begin{array}{r} 53¢ \\ +20¢ \\ \hline \boxed{73¢} \end{array} \qquad \begin{array}{r} 73 \\ -20 \\ \hline 53 \end{array}$$

Carlos started out with 73¢.

Explain how you solved the problem.

I solved this problem by working backwards and taking what I know and just pretended that he never spent anything and just put what he had left and what he spent together.

FIGURE 11–1 The student begins with the 53¢ Carlos has left and adds the 20¢ previously spent to find an answer.

Baseball Cards

David bought some baseball cards. He gave half of the cards he bought to Tyvone. Then he gave half of what he had left to Sherri. After that he had 12 cards. How many cards did he buy?

Ended having only 12 cards × 2 being the half Sherri got = 24 cards now × 2 being the half Tyvone recieved = 48 total cards to begin with.

Explain how you solved the problem.

To solve this problem I first started at the end of the problem because I knew I'd be working backwards. I found out he (David) started with 12 baseball cards. Then, I read that he (David) had given Sherri half, so I doubled 12 and got 24. Now, I read the last clue and it said that David had given Tyvone half of that, so I doubled 24 and got 48 and so I came to the conclusion that he had bought 48 baseball cards to begin with.

FIGURE 11–2 This problem begins with David giving away half of his cards. To determine how many cards David started with, the student must work backward to determine the value of "half."

Preparing for the Big Snow

Mrs. Pinson went to the grocery store to get ready for the big snow. First, she spent half of her money on food. Then, she spent $6.30 on some logs for the fire. On the way home, she spent another $15.00 to fill her car with gas. When she got home, she had $20.00 left. How much did Mrs. Pinson have at the start?

$82.60

Which strategy would you choose to solve this problem? Why?

Working Backwards. I selected this one because the first peice of info is at the end.

Solve the problem and explain how you arrived at your answer.

$$\begin{array}{r} \$20.00 - \text{the amount of money she had left} \\ +\$15.00 - \text{amount she spend on gas} \\ \hline 35.00 \\ +\ 6.30 - \text{amount she spent on fire logs} \\ \hline \$41.30 \\ \times\ \ 2 \\ \hline \$82.60 - \text{amount of money she started off with} \end{array}$$

The stratagey I used to get my answer is working backwards. To get my answer I first wrote down the amount she had left and added it to the amounts that she had spent. The last thing I did was multiply my total by "2" because it said she spent half in the grocery store and that meant I only had half of what she spent when I got the total; so I had to multiply by "2" to get the actual amount she spent. That is how I figured out how much she started with.

---

reversing the operations as they work backward. After they master reversing the operations, students can be challenged by such terms as *half* or *one-third* (see Figure 11–2).

Analyzing students' writing allows you to see if they have mastered the working-backward process. (see Figure 11–3.)

FIGURE 11–3 This student's writing reflects an understanding of the work-backward strategy.

Reflecting on the Strategy

Remember to have students write and talk about the strategy they used to solve the problem. Try prompts like these:

▌ How did working backward help you solve this problem?

▌ Explain to a friend who has never tried this strategy how he or she can work backward to solve a problem.

▌ Why is working backward a good strategy for solving this problem?

▌ Why is it important to check your work after solving a problem using the Work Backward strategy?

CHAPTER TWELVE

Real-World Problem Solving

The excitement of learning and applying mathematics is generated when problems develop within the context of a situation familiar to students. Allowing them to formulate problems as they naturally arise within the context of everyday experiences gives them the opportunity to put mathematics to work, observing its usefulness and its applicability.

Judith S. Zawojewski

The goal of problem-solving instruction is to have students build a repertoire of strategies with which they can solve real problems. Through practice with real-world tasks, they begin to develop their abilities to apply problem-solving strategies. In addition, they begin to see the value in learning the skills and processes needed to become successful problem solvers. The NCTM's *Curriculum and Evaluation Standards for School Mathematics* states "Students need to see when and how mathematics can be used, rather than be promised that someday they will use it!" (35). Having students engage in problem-solving activities using real data from authentic materials, such as the newspaper, travel brochures, menus, or catalogs, will naturally show the connection between classroom skills and the application of those skills. Students will begin to see that problem solving occurs outside the math classroom, too.

Creating Meaningful Real-World Tasks

Although activities using real-world materials have been used in math classes for years, these activities have traditionally focused on calculation skills, as in the following menu problem:

Mary Elizabeth bought a hamburger for $1.25. She paid for it with a $5.00 bill. How much change did she receive?

In this problem, there is one correct answer: $3.75. The student is either right or wrong. In today's problem-solving classrooms, teachers are encouraged to develop problems that require students to employ more reasoning and thought when solving problems. This often means that problems become open-ended and individual students' answers may vary. An open-ended question using a restaurant menu might be:

You and a friend will be ordering lunch. You have $10.00 to spend. What will you and your friend order? How much change will you receive?

In this problem, students are still required to subtract to find their change. But, students now must work together to decide what they will order. Students first use their number sense and estimation skills to select some items to order. After adding their totals, they may need to adjust their decisions, as they may have overspent, or they may find that they have extra money and decide to add to their order. This problem provides practice with basic operations, but also stimulates thinking and encourages communication. Each student pair may have a different, but correct, answer. In the process of solving the problem, students will have practiced their reasoning, calculating, and communicating skills.

Problems involving a restaurant menu will also allow students to exercise and refine their reasoning skills by examining daily specials to determine if they are truly "deals." One local children's menu offered Kids' Meal Deals for $3.49. The Kids' Meal Deals included the regular meal, a drink, and a dessert. Students were asked to determine if this was truly a good buy. It is obvious from the third grader's response below that not only did she practice many calculations in her attempt to find the solution, but she employed her reasoning skills as well. The student first decided to calculate the cost for a variety of meal combinations when purchased separately, including the highest-priced meal with the highest-priced drink and dessert and the lowest-priced meal with the lowest-priced drink and dessert. After many calculations, she determined that even the lowest priced meal, drink, and desert were more expensive than the Kids' Meal Deal. In her own way, she justifies her solution as follows:

"Kids' Meal Deals is a better deal because its less than the regular meal and a drink and a dessert. The highest with regular prices is

$5.09. The lowest with regular prices is $3.69 and that's higher than the meal deal. You get the same food and it's less money."

She came up with a reasonable answer, and after discussions with classmates, she realized that she hadn't needed to calculate the cost of the higher-priced combinations in order to answer the question. The revelation that using just the lowest-priced items would yield the solution was the result of conversations with classmates and thoughtful review of the problem. When asked how she would change her strategy next time, she asserted that starting with the cheapest meal would be best because she might not have to do as much adding. (And she was right!)

Applying Classroom Skills to Meaningful Tasks

Investigations, which require students to incorporate thinking skills along with arithmetic skills, serve to challenge students. Consider the following task that challenges students to apply their skills in choosing the correct operation to a real-world situation. Fourth-grade students who had developed an understanding of key concepts for the operations through a series of classroom practice activities were asked to use their knowledge to determine the savings for purchasing festival tickets in advance. Students were given a brochure for a festival held each year in their local area (see Figure 12–1). They were asked to plan a family trip to the festival and calculate how much money they would save if they bought their tickets in advance.

Students first needed to calculate the cost of admission based on the Advanced Purchase ticket information on the brochure. In order to solve this first part of the task, students needed to *multiply* the number of adult tickets they were buying by the cost for each adult ticket, since each adult ticket cost the same amount (requires knowledge of the concept of multiplication). They also used *multiplication* to calculate the cost of senior and child tickets if more than one of either type

Discount Ticket Offer

Buy Now and Save!

Regular Price	Advanced Purchase	Cost
Adult (16–61) $11.95	_____ Tickets at $10.00	_____
Senior (62+) . . . .$ 9.95	_____ Tickets at $ 9.00	_____
Child (7–15) . . . .$ 4.95	_____ Tickets at $ 4.00	_____
Under 7 . . . . .free		
	Total Cost	_____

FIGURE 12–1   This brochure offers real data that allows students to practice their problem-solving skills.

was purchased. Then they had to *add* the cost of adult, senior, and child tickets to find their total cost, since each price was different (requires knowledge of the concept of addition).

After calculating the cost for their trip if tickets were purchased in advance, students had to recalculate the total cost using the regular admission prices, again using multiplication and addition when appropriate. In addition, they needed to use *subtraction*, since students were *comparing* the total cost of advance tickets to the total cost of tickets purchased at the door. This activity asked students to use their knowledge of key concepts to solve a problem that required them to perform several operations prior to coming up with the solution.

Student writing is helpful in analyzing students' understanding of the final step in the problem—determining how much they would save if they purchased tickets in advance.

"I figured it out by subtracting the advance purchase price from the regular price and got $2.90. I subtracted because I compared numbers and that's when you subtract. I could see how much more one was than the other."

Dependent on how many family members went to the festival and what their ages were, the students' savings differed. Each answer related specifically to each student's own data. In solving the problem for his or her family, each child was able to apply the math he or

she knew to a real-world situation that related to him or her.

Similar problems can be developed from attraction brochures from amusement parks, zoos, museums, or water parks. Often, these attractions have special admission deals that are perfect for real-world problem solving. Consider attractions that offer individual admission rates and a family rate. You could ask students to determine if entering under the family rate would make sense for their family. Water parks and amusement parks often offer season passes. You could ask students to determine the number of visits they would need to make to the attraction in order to make the season pass the best buy, which would encourage reasoning while offering arithmetic practice. Family rates, special discounts, season passes, and consecutive-day savings all offer ideas for real-world problem-solving activities.

Utilizing the Messiness of Real-World Data

Unlike textbook word problems, real-world problems are not always clear-cut, easily defined, and composed of simple numbers. "Situations that allow students to experience problems with 'messy' numbers or too much or not enough information or that have multiple solutions, each with different consequences, will better prepare them to solve problems they are likely to encounter in their daily lives" (NCTM 1989, 76). When students use grocery ads to select items for a Thanksgiving meal, they may be faced with buying items that are sold by weight or in packages or sets, for example, six soft drinks to a pack. This real-world data causes students to stop and consider how to proceed in solving the problem. Throughout the problem-solving situation, students must be aware of the data and make decisions based on how the data is presented in the real-world material.

There are 10 dinner guests, but soft drinks are sold in multiples of 6—what should you do?

You need 1 pound of turkey per person, but will you find a turkey that weighs exactly 10 pounds?

Students are faced with making sense of real data as they attempt to solve the problem, preparing them for future problem-solving experiences in a way that textbooks and worksheets are unable to do.

Discovering a World of Real Data

Real-world materials can be found everywhere. As you become aware of the role that real-world materials can play in your classroom, you will discover an abundance of materials that will motivate your students and provide meaningful, authentic mathematics explorations.

Newspapers
The daily newspaper is the most versatile real-world material because of its accessibility, affordability, and the variety of its data. Just one newspaper contains numerous examples of mathematics in action. Data is printed from the first page to the last, and you can use one issue for weeks without reusing a single article or piece of data. The currency of the newspaper allows teachers to capitalize on "what's hot" with articles about popular people such as politicians, rock stars, or sports heroes; current sporting activities such as the Olympics, or major league play-offs; or world events

such as political elections or natural disasters. The newspaper is also very affordable. Many newspapers offer educator discounts that will enable you to purchase inexpensive classroom sets of newspapers for use with your students.

The variety of mathematics represented throughout its pages makes the newspaper an obvious reflection of the magnitude by which mathematics affects all parts of our lives. Each section of the newspaper contains unique information that reinforces a variety of skills. The daily weather section offers data about local weather and usually contains information about weather in other parts of the country and the world. The sports section provides game and player statistics and various tables that show team standings and statistics. You may find diagrams of sports fields, tables comparing player or team statistics, and graphs that reflect sports data. Travel sections contain cost information for hotels or airfare to travel destinations. In addition, these sections frequently contain maps, complete with a map scale, to show the distances when traveling from one location to another. Amusement sections offer times and prices for a variety of entertainment events, and business sections provide a variety of graphs that your students can analyze. Classified advertisement sections include the cost information for placing ads, which allows students to calculate the cost of existing ads or write their own ads and determine the cost of running them in the newspaper. Newspapers often include food sections with recipes or home sections with home-improvement designs, including measurements. And all newspapers contain numerous advertisements. Ads for clothing, housewares, cars, jewelry, toys, or furniture can be found throughout the paper. Grocery ads also appear in the newspaper and provide data for a variety of activities including finding the best buys, estimating the cost of a grocery list, or planning refreshments for a party or family outing.

The variety of data appearing in the newspaper, combined with the material's affordability and accessibility, makes it a rich resource for classroom teachers. In addition, because it is a consumable (discardable) resource, teachers can create hands-on lessons that allow students to circle, cut, or paste newspaper articles or data. The ability to cut, mark, or paste transforms the newspaper into a hands-on tool, allowing students to be actively involved in a variety of math projects and investigations.

Restaurant Menus

Restaurant menus particularly children's menus, which are available in many restaurants, are readily accessible real-world materials. The children's menus are often printed separately from the main menu and are sometimes given to children as placemats or coloring papers. They may be reproducible, with the restaurant's permission and some restaurants are willing to donate a set to teachers on request. Some ideas for menu activities can be found in Appendix H.

Recipes

Teachers can select recipes from cookbooks or ask students to bring in favorite recipes from home. Children's cookbooks often contain recipes with "kid appeal" that can be used to create highly motivating classroom activities. Recipe problem-solving activities require students to manipulate the data in the recipe in order to solve the problem. Teachers could ask students to reduce or enlarge a recipe based on the number of people who will be served. They may be asked to formulate the grocery store list based on the ingredients needed to make the recipe. They could ask students to use their reasoning skills to determine the fewest number of measuring cups and spoons that can be used while still being sure that measurements are exact. Some ideas for kid-friendly recipe books are available in Appendix H.

Travel Brochures

Travel brochures are usually colorful, inviting, and filled with math data. Brochures from attractions that appeal to children will provide instant motivation for students to jump into an activity. Brochures from amusement parks, museums, historical sites related to social studies units, or local attractions that are popular with students contain high-interest data. Calculating admission costs for a family or a class, deciding on a schedule for visiting specific events when times are listed on the brochure, and calculating mileage to and from the location when a map with map scale is available are examples of some real-world math tasks that come to life with travel brochures. See Appendix H for more ideas on travel activities.

Travel brochures are available at the attractions themselves and are usually free of charge. Most attractions will be happy to give you multiple copies if they are available. Remember that students are encouraged to work together on problem-solving activities, so a brochure for each student is unnecessary. Depending on the task, teachers may only need a brochure for each group of two, three, or four students in the class. Brochures may also be obtained by writing to the individual attractions and requesting information. You can obtain addresses and phone numbers for local attractions by writing to, telephoning, or e-mailing individual state tourist board offices. A list of Internet addresses and telephone numbers for state tourist boards is included in Appendix H. Visitor centers on the interstates or hotel lobbies are great places to browse through brochures to find ones that are just right for your class.

Catalogs

Catalogs from sporting goods companies, clothing companies, and toy stores offer lots of interesting data for problem-solving activities. Because catalogs (unlike textbooks) are consumable, students can cut out pictures of the items they wish to purchase and include the pictures with their mathematical data. Students can create tables to show the items purchased, including prices and quantities. Teachers can ask students to select several pieces of clothing from a clothing catalog and make an organized list to show how many different outfits can be created. Students can construct tables to determine how much it would cost to buy one, two, three, four, or five of an item. Students may need to calculate shipping and handling charges which often requires knowledge of percents and are often dependent on the total cost of the order. Catalogs are generally free and companies may be willing to send you duplicate sets if they know you will be using them in the classroom. In addition, parents are often willing to donate outdated catalogs from home.

Grocery Ads

Most major grocery stores run specials each week. These specials are advertised in grocery ads that are inserted into newspapers or sent out through the mail. In addition, most stores have copies available for pickup as you enter the store. The ads are filled with price data and usually include pictures or graphics. There are lots of intriguing possibilities for math problems using data about food that is sold by weight, food that is sold in packs (e.g., six sodas in a pack), or food that is sold per item.

Teachers might ask students to use the ads to plan menus for parties or family events. They could ask students to select any item that costs less than 50 cents and then list all the possible coin combinations they might use to buy the item. Coupon shopping, combining clipped coupons and grocery ad prices, allows children to calculate the final cost of items that are purchased using coupons.

Students can be asked to bring in ads from home, or teachers can visit grocery stores on the last day of the advertised specials. Store managers are usually quite willing to give away the old ads when new ones are ready to take their place on the store shelves.

Sports Schedules

Local sports teams often publicize their schedules on free handouts. These schedules usually contain a series of calendars showing dates for home and away games, game times, and special promotion nights. Often, they also contain price information. The schedules can be used to plan imaginary outings to the sports events and calculate the cost of admissions. Calls to local teams should be all that is needed to get a copy of the current team schedule.

Sports Player Cards

Children have collected and traded baseball cards for years, and now football, basketball, and hockey cards are also available for trading and collecting. Each card is filled with data about a specific player. Students can compare players' performances, rank players based on statistics on their cards, or trade players to create a "dream team" based on the data on the cards. Logical reasoning games can be created using card data like the following game in which students were given data from several players and asked to find the right player based on the clues:

- I have a batting average that is better than .300.
- I hit an even number of home runs last year.
- My number of hits is a multiple of 5.
- **Who am I?**

Or, you could have students work with partners and write clues to help their partners determine the number of singles, triples, or home runs hit by their player. Following is an example:

- He hit more than 20 home runs.
- It is an even number.
- It is a multiple of 6.
- It is less than 25.
- **How many home runs did he hit?**

The fun of actually being able to handle the cards, combined with the colorful photos on each card, makes the data more inviting than similar data that can be taken from a newspaper column. Player cards range in prices depending on whether they are the economy models or part of an exclusive series. For classroom activities, the inexpensive cards, work well. Students can donate their old cards, or you can purchase inexpensive cards from local stores.

Nutritional Labels

Nutritional labels are on all types of food—the trick is to select foods that will appeal to students. Comparing the sugar or fat content in their favorite cookies may be more motivating than looking at the fat content of lima beans. Students could use tables to determine the grams of fat in eight cookies, if the label indicates that there are three grams of fat in two cookies. Students might be given five food labels and be asked to use the Guess, Check, and Revise strategy to determine which three items they ate, knowing that they ate fourteen total grams of fat.

Students can collect labels from home and bring them to school. Teachers may want to have a box in their classroom in which students place the labels when they bring the labels in from home. It may be helpful to have index cards available so students can glue the labels to the cards and write the name of the food product on the card. Cards can then be sorted by food category for storage until you plan to use them.

Advertisements

A variety of advertisements, often in a magazine format, are often inserted in daily newspapers or received in households from mass mailings. Ads are available from a variety of stores including toy stores, department stores, drug stores, computer stores, or specialty shops. The ads usually list sale prices, sometimes calculated as half off or 20 percent off. Often the original prices are listed. Students can select gifts for their families or put together a birthday "wish list." Students could use the original and sale prices to determine the percentage of the original price that they are paying. You might select several items from one page in the catalog and then calculate the total cost of purchasing the items. Give students the total cost of the items and have them use the Guess, Check, and Revise strategy to determine which items you bought from that page. Students could use advertised prices to determine reasonable exchanges. If they are returning an item that costs $21.95, have them decide which items they will get in exchange. Students can bring in ads from home or teachers can inquire at stores for multiple copies. You may only need one copy so that the class can share the data.

Reaping the Benefit of Real-World Activities

Through open-ended investigations that require students to use real-world data, students will begin to view the mathematics they learn in class as a meaningful skill that connects to many areas of their lives. Along with giving students the opportunity to apply classroom skills, the open-ended problem-solving format offers students an opportunity to communicate about their mathematical thinking through group work and discussions. These investigations require students to use their reasoning skills to formulate plans and determine effective strategies for solving the investigations. Whether they are simple problems or more complex tasks, they direct students' attention to the everyday applications of mathematics.

Real-world materials are everywhere. The more that you gather, the more you will discover. Stay focused on the NCTM Standards and the problem-solving strategies presented in this book to help you keep on track with your activities so that you develop not only fun activities, but activities that move students toward the math goals that you have set for them.

CHAPTER THIRTEEN

Accepting the Challenge

Improving the teaching of mathematics depends on what the teacher

knows and does.   NCTM, Professional Standards for Teaching

Mathematics

The Challenge to Educators

Teaching students to become effective problem solvers is both the goal and the challenge of elementary mathematics instruction. Educators are beginning to recognize that problem-solving skills can and should be systematically taught to students. Experts have identified checklists and strategies that guide students through the problem-solving process and assist them in organizing needed data. Discussions, group work, and writing in mathematics class have allowed students to share their thinking processes and strengthen their understanding of the skills they are acquiring. And the integration of real-world data into the math classroom has challenged students to apply problem-solving skills to real situations.

As the central focus of the mathematics curriculum, problem solving must be systematically taught, and problem-solving experiences must become a part of your daily mathematics instruction. Through the development of a positive classroom climate, you will allow your students to test their skills and extend their thinking in a safe, comfortable

environment that supports risk taking and creative thinking. Through hands-on and visual teaching techniques, you will enable your students to acquire knowledge in problem-solving processes and strategies and begin to build a repertoire of strategies and skills to allow them to tackle even complex problems. Through a variety of practice activities, your students will be able to extend and refine their skills, and through the introduction of real-world activities, you will give your students opportunities to apply their knowledge to meaningful tasks.

Your goal as a math educator should be to acquire skills and strategies to help your students grow as mathematical thinkers. You are challenged to experiment with new strategies and techniques within your classroom to allow students to visualize and experience problem-solving situations. You are challenged to encourage students to communicate their ideas, discuss alternate solutions, and monitor their own thinking processes. You are challenged to stimulate students with thought-provoking, open-ended problems and guide your students toward reasonable solutions.

You are challenged to connect students' classroom skills to meaningful real-world tasks, providing students with opportunities to apply their knowledge. You are challenged to create a classroom in which students investigate, explore, reason, and communicate about problem solving on a daily basis and in which they can grow to become confident and capable problem solvers.

Appendix A
Problem-Solving Checklists

Problem-Solving Checklist

Understand the Question
What is the problem you are being asked to solve?

Choose a Plan
What strategy will you use to solve the problem?
What do you think the answer will be?

Try Your Plan
Try your strategy to solve the problem.

Check Your Answer
Does your answer make sense?
Are your calculations correct?

Reflect on What You've Done
Why did you pick the strategy you did?

Problem-Solving Checklist

Understand the Question
What is the problem you are being asked to solve?

Choose a Plan
What strategy will you use to solve the problem?
What do you think the answer will be?

Try Your Plan
Try your strategy to solve the problem.

Check Your Answer
Does your answer make sense?
Are your calculations correct?

Reflect on What You've Done
What was easy about solving this problem?
What was hard?

Appendix B
Key Concepts Posters

Put together.

KEY CONCEPTS POSTERS

Take away.

Compare.

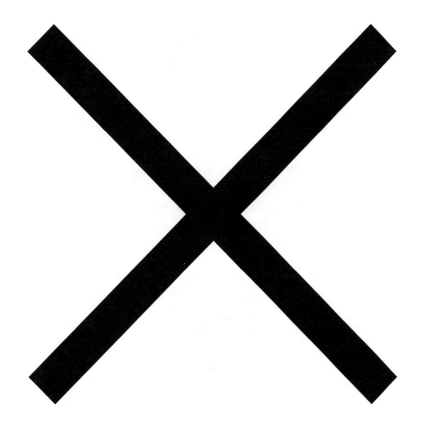

Put together.

(equal sets)

Separate into groups.

How many in each group?

How many groups?

Appendix C
Observation Checklist

Problem-Solving Group Observation Checklist

Group members:

_____

_____

_____

Key:
(+) behavior observed
(–) negative/opposing behavior observed
(n/a) no opportunity for observing this behavior

_____ All group members were involved in the task.

_____ Group members were able to verbalize the problem in their own words.

_____ Group members helped one another understand the problem and possible solutions.

_____ Group members were able to decide on a reasonable plan for solving the problem.

_____ Group members worked together to execute their plan.

_____ Group members checked the reasonableness and accuracy of their solution.

_____ Group members were able to explain the process they used to solve the problem.

Appendix D
Assessment Tools

Holistic Rubric
for Scoring Problem Solving

Expected Student Outcomes:
Students will be able to
  1. select and use an appropriate strategy.
  2. calculate a correct answer.
  3. explain their strategy for solving the problem.

Problem-Solving Rubric:
4 – arrived at a correct answer; used an appropriate strategy; adequately explained answer
3 – used an appropriate strategy; calculated a correct answer but could not explain the strategy; *or* adequately explained the strategy but did not calculate a correct answer
2 – used an appropriate strategy; did not find a correct answer; could not explain the strategy
1 – attempted to solve the problem, but completely incorrect in attempt
0 – no attempt/blank

Name _____ Date _____

Evaluating My Problem Solving

Carefully look over your corrected paper and answer the questions below.

I used a strategy that made sense. yes   no

I got the correct answer. yes   no

I explained my strategy. yes   no

My score was _____.

Next time I will improve my work by

_____

_____

_____

_____

Reflecting on Problem Solving

Reflections will help teachers identify students' feelings about problem solving as well as their perceived strengths and weaknesses and their confusions about problem-solving lessons. Students might answer one or several prompts each week in a problem-solving journal. Encouraging students to look back over past entries will help them monitor their growth as problem solvers. Try the following:

When a problem is hard, I . . .
The easiest part of problem solving is . . .
The hardest part of problem solving is . . .
I'm confused about . . .
Now I understand . . .
The most important thing I learned today is . . .
I can use what I learned today when I . . .
When I don't know what to do I . . .
I discovered that . . .
When I work with a partner I feel . . .
When I work with a group I feel . . .
I need help on . . .
I'm glad I know how to . . .
I get frustrated when . . .
Something I learned today that will be very useful is . . .
The strategy I am best at is . . .
The strategy that I'm confused about is . . .
If I could hear one lesson over again it would be . . .

Appendix E
Pinch Cards

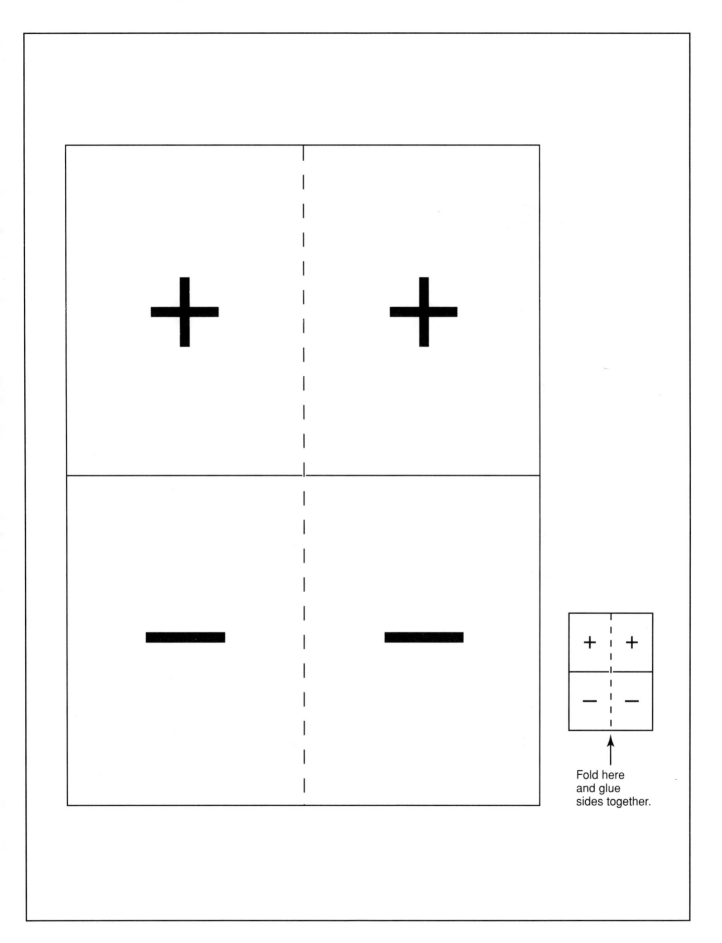

Fold here
and glue
sides together.

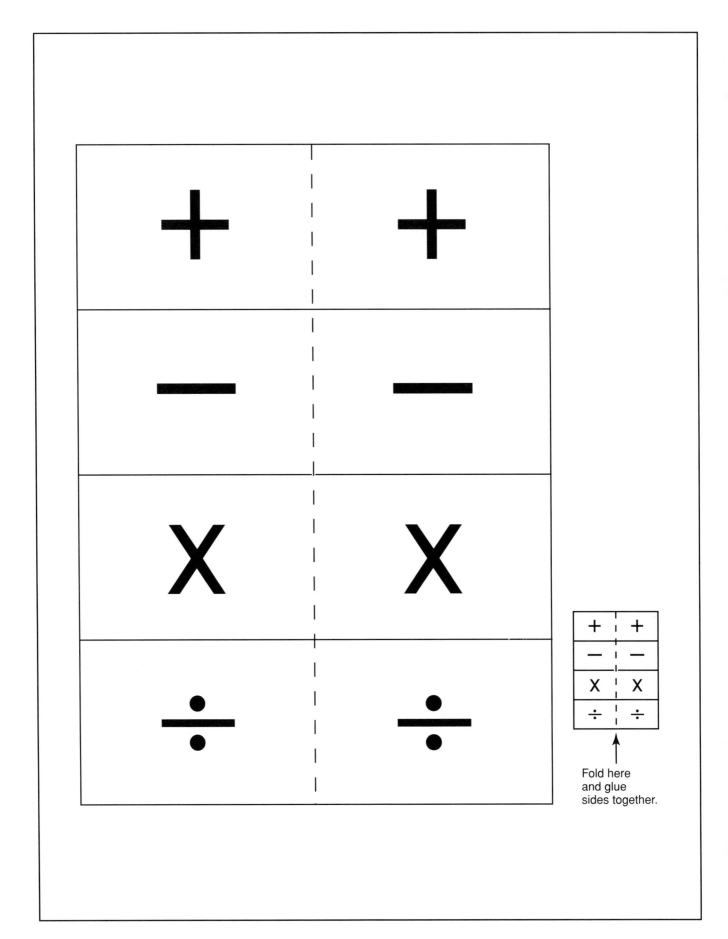

Fold here
and glue
sides together.

Appendix F
Strategy Icons

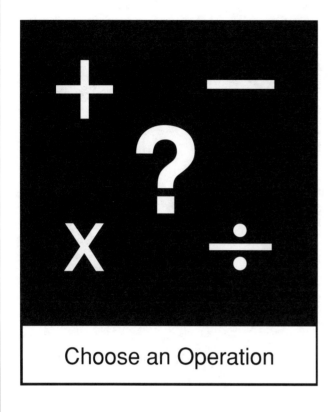

Choose an Operation

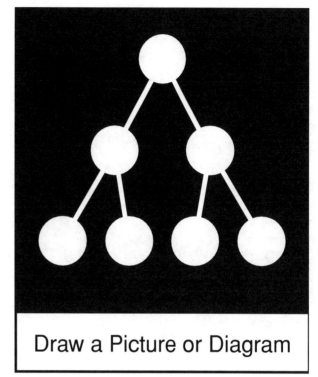

Draw a Picture or Diagram

Guess, Check and Revise

Make an Organized List

Find a Pattern

Use Logical Reasoning

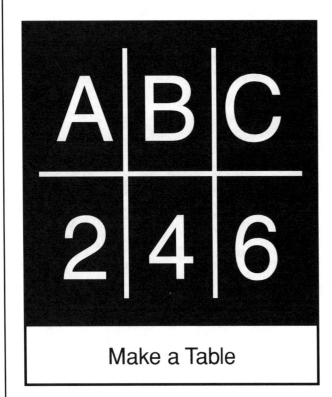

Make a Table

Work Backward

Appendix G
Practice Problems

Following are some problems that might be solved by using the strategies presented in this book. Remember that there is often more than one appropriate strategy to solve a problem. Although the highlighted strategy would be a logical and appropriate strategy for any of the problems in the section, teachers must look at each child's strategy and determine if it is appropriate for the problem.

The problems range from simple to complex. Select those that are appropriate for your students or modify the problems to fit your students' abilities either by changing the numbers or by adding or deleting some variables.

For each problem, students are asked to explain their thinking or justify their solutions in writing. This will help you get a clearer picture of what they were thinking during the problem-solving process.

Find a Pattern Practice Problems

1–100 Charts

1	2	3	4	5	6	7	8	9	10
11	12	13	14	15	16	17	18	19	20
21	22	23	24	25	26	27	28	29	30
31	32	33	34	35	36	37	38	39	40
41	42	43	44	45	46	47	48	49	50
51	52	53	54	55	56	57	58	59	60
61	62	63	64	65	66	67	68	69	70
71	72	73	74	75	76	77	78	79	80
81	82	83	84	85	86	87	88	89	90
91	92	93	94	95	96	97	98	99	100

1	2	3	4	5	6	7	8	9	10
11	12	13	14	15	16	17	18	19	20
21	22	23	24	25	26	27	28	29	30
31	32	33	34	35	36	37	38	39	40
41	42	43	44	45	46	47	48	49	50
51	52	53	54	55	56	57	58	59	60
61	62	63	64	65	66	67	68	69	70
71	72	73	74	75	76	77	78	79	80
81	82	83	84	85	86	87	88	89	90
91	92	93	94	95	96	97	98	99	100

1	2	3	4	5	6	7	8	9	10
11	12	13	14	15	16	17	18	19	20
21	22	23	24	25	26	27	28	29	30
31	32	33	34	35	36	37	38	39	40
41	42	43	44	45	46	47	48	49	50
51	52	53	54	55	56	57	58	59	60
61	62	63	64	65	66	67	68	69	70
71	72	73	74	75	76	77	78	79	80
81	82	83	84	85	86	87	88	89	90
91	92	93	94	95	96	97	98	99	100

1	2	3	4	5	6	7	8	9	10
11	12	13	14	15	16	17	18	19	20
21	22	23	24	25	26	27	28	29	30
31	32	33	34	35	36	37	38	39	40
41	42	43	44	45	46	47	48	49	50
51	52	53	54	55	56	57	58	59	60
61	62	63	64	65	66	67	68	69	70
71	72	73	74	75	76	77	78	79	80
81	82	83	84	85	86	87	88	89	90
91	92	93	94	95	96	97	98	99	100

Hundred Chart

1	2	3	4	5	6	7	8	9	10
11	12	13	14	15	16	17	18	19	20
21	22	23	24	25	26	27	28	29	30
31	32	33	34	35	36	37	38	39	40
41	42	43	44	45	46	47	48	49	50
51	52	53	54	55	56	57	58	59	60
61	62	63	64	65	66	67	68	69	70
71	72	73	74	75	76	77	78	79	80
81	82	83	84	85	86	87	88	89	90
91	92	93	94	95	96	97	98	99	100

Name _____ Date _____

What's the Score?

In a video game, the first score was worth 1 point. The second score was worth 3 points. The third score was worth 5 points. How much was the eighth score worth?

Describe the pattern that helped you solve this problem.

Name _____ Date _____

Win a Prize

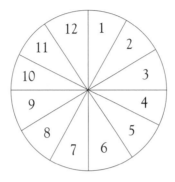

At the school carnival, there was a prize wheel. Each student got to spin the wheel one time to see if he or she won a prize. Spinning a "one" won a prize. Spinning a "two" or "three" did not win anything. Spinning a "four" won a prize. Spinning a "five" or "six" did not win anything. Spinning a "seven" won a prize, and so forth. Rita spun a "twelve." Did she win a prize?

Explain how you figured out the answer.

Name _____ Date _____

Treats at the Mall

The mall was having a special "Celebrate Children" month. Each day, it gave a special treat to children who came to the mall to shop with their parents. On Oct. 1, it gave each child a cookie; on the 2nd, it gave away candy; on the 3rd, it gave away balloons; on the 4th, it gave away cookies; on the 5th, it gave away candy; and on the 6th, it gave away balloons. What did each child receive on Oct. 30?

Explain how you solved the problem.

Name _____ Date _____

Soccer Practice

Katie's soccer coach was trying to get the team in shape for the season. On the first day of practice, she made them run one lap around the field. On the second day, she made them run three laps. On the third day, they ran five laps, and on the fourth day they ran seven laps. How many laps did the coach make them run on the fifth day of practice?

They ran _____ laps.

Describe the pattern.

How did knowing the pattern help you solve the problem?

Name _____ Date _____

The Lineup

The students were lined up for the school concert. The teacher lined them up one girl, then two boys, then one girl, then two boys. If there were twenty children in line, how many were girls?

Explain how you solved the problem.

Name _____ Date _____

A Border of Hearts

Amy was helping her mom put a wallpaper border in her bedroom. The border had a row of hearts: one yellow, then two red, then one pink, then the pattern repeated. When she was finished, there was a row of 25 hearts around her room. How many pink hearts were there?

How did knowing the pattern help you solve the problem?

Name _____ Date _____

The Jelly Bean Jar

Lisa had a jar of jelly beans on her desk. The first time she dipped her hand into the jar, she took one jelly bean. The next time, she took three jelly beans. On her third trip to the candy jar, she took six jelly beans. Then she took ten jelly beans from the jar. How many jelly beans do you think she took on her fifth trip to the jar?

Explain how you decided on your answer.

Name _____ Date _____

The Race

Andrew ran a 6-mile race. He ran the first mile in 7 minutes. The second mile took him 7½ minutes to run. He ran the third mile in 8 minutes, and the fourth mile in 8½ minutes. Use the pattern to help you figure out how long it took him to complete the entire race.

Andrew ran the entire race in _____ minutes.

Describe the pattern in the problem.

How did knowing the pattern help you figure out the answer?

Making Tables Practice Problems

Peanut Butter Prices

You can buy 2 jars of peanut butter for 3 dollars. How much will it cost to buy 6 jars of peanut butter? Finish the table to help you figure out the answer.

jars of peanut butter					
dollars					

Circle the answer on your table.

Do you see any patterns on your table? Describe one pattern.

Name _____ Date _____

Birthday Balloons

At Jenny's birthday party, each guest received 3 balloons in his or her treat bag. How many balloons did Jenny need to buy to fill 7 treat bags?

Explain the strategy you used to solve the problem.

Name _____ Date _____

Go-Kart Costs

It costs $1.50 to go 2 laps at the Go-Kart Track. How much will it cost to go 8 laps?

Explain how making a table might help you solve this problem.

Name _____ Date _____

How Many Lemons?

Ellen used 4 lemons to make a 3-liter pitcher of lemonade. How many lemons will she need in order to make 24 liters of lemonade for the picnic?

Explain the strategy you used to solve this problem.

Name _____ Date _____

Jump Up

Alice jumps rope faster than anyone in her class. She can jump 8 times in 4 seconds. How long will it take her to jump 40 times?

Explain the strategy you used to solve this problem.

Name _____ Date _____

Creative Cookies

Erica was decorating gingerbread cookies with raisins for eyes, a marshmallow for a nose, and a row of 4 peanuts to make a mouth. How many of each item will she need to decorate 8 cookies?

Why is making a table a good strategy for solving this problem?

Name _____ Date _____

Cans of Cola

A six-pack of cola costs $2.50. How many cans of cola can Jason buy with $12.50?

Explain the strategy you used to solve the problem.

Name _____ Date _____

Student Supplies

For the math activity, each student needed one ruler, three strips of paper, and four paper clips. How many rulers, strips of paper, and paper clips were needed for a group of six students?

Explain the strategy you used to solve this problem.

Name _____ Date _____

The Bake Sale

Katie was baking cookies for the school bake sale. She needed 2 eggs to make one dozen cookies. How many eggs will she need if she wants to bake 60 cookies?

Explain how you solved the problem.

Name _____ Date _____

Trick-or-Treat

Allison went shopping to buy trick-or-treat candy. Each bag of candy costs $2.69. How many bags could she buy with $10.00?

Explain how you solved the problem.

Name _____ Date _____

Video Savings

1. Joe wants to buy a video game for $39.00. He gets $7.00 each week for his allowance. How many weeks will it take for Joe to save enough of his allowance money to buy the video game?

2. If Joe started with $13.00 in his savings, how many weeks would it take him to have enough money to buy the game?

Explain how you solved the second problem.

Make an Organized List
Practice Problems

Drinks and Cookies
Manipulative Sheet

Name _____ Date _____

Making Valentines

Imagine that you decide to make valentines for your friends. You can cut the paper into three shapes—round, square, or heart-shaped. You can decorate them with stripes or polka dots. How many different kinds of valentines can you make?

____ valentines

Show how you solved the problem.

Name _____ Date _____

Snowy Snacks

After playing in the snow, Joe decided to go inside and have a snack. He could have hot chocolate, milk, or cola to drink. He could have pretzels, cookies, or raisins to eat. How many food/drink combinations are possible?

Explain how you solved the problem.

Name _____ Date _____

Buying Bagels

Mrs. Whittles bought bagels for her family. She bought wheat, onion, and cinnamon bagels. She bought vegetable and plain cream cheese. How many bagel/cream cheese combinations are there?

Explain the strategy you used to solve this problem.

Name _____ Date _____

Lunch Choices

Pat wanted to make a sandwich for lunch. He had white and wheat bread. He had ham, turkey, and peanut butter. How many different kinds of sandwiches (one type of bread and one type of filling) could Pat make?

How can you be sure that you found all the possible sandwich combinations?

Name _____ Date _____

Shoes and Socks

Erica has red and white shoes. She has blue, green, pink, and yellow socks. How many different shoe/sock combinations can she make? (No mismatched shoes or socks allowed!)

Are you sure that you wrote down all the possible combinations? Why?

Name _____ Date _____

Delicious Desserts

Mrs. Haney can order apple, peach, or cherry pie. She can have either vanilla ice cream or whipped cream on her pie, or no topping at all. How many choices does she have?

Explain how you know your answer is correct.

Name _____ Date _____

Chicken Delight

Jessica's family brought her to dinner to celebrate her great report card. They went to Chicken Delight, where each dinner includes a meat, a vegetable, and a bread.

Meats	**Vegetables**	**Breads**
chicken	peas	rolls
ham	green beans	corn bread
	carrots	

How many different dinner combinations does Jessica have to choose from?

Explain the strategy you used to solve the problem.

Name _____ Date _____

Amusement Park Fun

Michelle's family is going to Disney World. They want to ride on Space Mountain, It's a Small World, and Splash Mountain. They need to decide the order in which they will visit the attractions. How many different orders are possible?

Explain how you solved the problem.

Name _____ Date _____

Coin Combinations

Chris bought a newspaper for 25¢. How many different coin combinations were possible to pay for the newspaper with exact change?

Explain why it is important to keep your data organized when solving this problem.

Name _____ Date _____

Buying Snacks

Ellen wants to buy a snack in a snack machine that will take only quarters, dimes, and nickels. If each snack costs 35¢, and if she must use exact change, how many different combinations of coins could Ellen use to buy a snack?

Explain how you solved the problem.

Draw a Picture or Diagram
Practice Problems

Name _____ Date _____

Bags of Fruit

Katie has 3 bags of fruit. There are 2 apples and 1 banana in each bag. How many apples does Katie have? How many bananas does Katie have?

Explain how you solved this problem.

Name _____ Date _____

Sharing a Sub

Jean bought a very big submarine sandwich to share with her friends for lunch. She cut it into four pieces so that everyone could have some. How many cuts did she have to make?

_____ cuts

Explain how you solved this problem.

Name _____ Date _____

Who's in the Class?

There are 25 children in Miss Lanham's class. They sit in rows. There are 5 children in each row. There are 3 boys and 2 girls in each row. How many boys are in the class? How many girls?

Explain the strategy you used to solve this problem.

Name _____ Date _____

Family Fun

Pat, Jean, Kathleen, and Liz were members of the same family. Jean was younger than Pat. Pat was younger than Liz. Kathleen was older than Pat, but younger than Liz. Can you name the children in order from youngest to oldest?

How did a picture or diagram help you solve this problem?

Name _____ Date _____

Take a Seat

There are 4 round tables and 3 square tables in the library.
6 students can sit at each round table. 4 students can sit at each
square table. How many students can sit in the library altogether?

Explain the strategy you used to solve this problem.

Name _____ **Date** _____

The Snowman

Megan built a snowman. She put five buttons on her snowman. The red button was below the blue one. The green button was above the blue one. The yellow button was between the blue and red buttons. The purple button was just above the green one. Which button was in the middle?

Explain how a picture or diagram could help you solve this problem.

Name _____ Date _____

Penny's Pet Shop

In Penny's Pet Shop, 1/4 of the pets were dogs, 1/2 of the pets were cats, 1/8 of the pets were birds, and the rest were gerbils. There were 48 pets in all. How many of each type of pet were there?

Explain the strategy you used to solve this problem.

Name _____ Date _____

The Party Guests

Emily had a party. She invited two guests. Her guests each invited two guests, and then those guests each invited three guests. How many people were at Emily's party?

Explain the strategy you used to solve this problem.

Guess, Check, and Revise
Practice Problems

Name _____ Date _____

Stacking Snowballs

Colleen, Joe, and Kevin each made a pile of snowballs. Together they made 13 snowballs. Which three piles belong to the children?

Explain how you solved the problem.

The Candy Count

Sam's friends gave him 3 bags of candy. Altogether, he received 37 pieces of candy. Which types of candy did his friends give him?

Jelly beans—10 pieces in a bag
Gumdrops—11 pieces in a bag
Mints—13 pieces in a bag
Cinnamons—16 pieces in a bag
Chocolates—19 pieces in a bag

Explain the strategy you used to solve the problem.

Name _____ Date _____

Fast Food Fun

Ruby bought 2 items at her favorite fast-food restaurant. Together they cost $2.78. Which two items did she buy?

Cheeseburger	69¢
Chicken nuggets	$2.09
Jumbo burger	$1.99
Fries	89¢
Milk	79¢
Milk shake	99¢

Explain how the Guess, Check, and Revise strategy could help you find the answer to this problem.

Name _____ Date _____

The Picnic

Melissa brought 16 pieces of fruit to the picnic. There were twice as many apples as bananas and 1 more orange than apples. How many of each type of fruit did she bring?

Explain how you solved this problem.

Name _____ Date _____

Kim's Party

Kim wrote ten invitations to her birthday party. She put them in two stacks. One stack had two more than the other stack. How many were in each stack?

Explain how you solved this problem.

Name _____ Date _____

How Old Is Caroline?

Caroline's age this year is a multiple of 5. Next year, Caroline's age will be a multiple of 4. How old is Caroline now?

Justify your answer. How do you know it is correct? Are there any other correct answers?

Name _____ Date _____

Monopoly Money

Katie and Brendan played a game of Monopoly. When the game ended, Brendan had $120.00 more than Katie did. Together they had $840.00. How much did each person have?

Explain the strategy you used to solve this problem.

Name _____ Date _____

Name the Numbers

Three consecutive whole numbers add up to 54. What are they?

Explain how you solved this problem.

Name _____ Date _____

The Garden

A garden is twice as long as it is wide. Its perimeter is 30 feet. How long is it?

Explain how you solved this problem.

APPENDIX G

Name _____ Date _____

The Lunch Order

Mrs. Baird ordered a carry-out lunch from Antonio's Restaurant. She ordered a salad and a drink. She paid with a $10.00 bill and received $6.60 in change. Which type of salad and which size drink did she order?

She ordered a _____
and a _____.

SALADS
Dinner salad $1.50
Garden salad $2.50
Tuna salad $2.99
Chef's salad $3.49
Turkey Salad $3.99

DRINKS
12 oz. - $.60
16 oz. - $.75
20 oz. - $.90

Explain the strategy you used to solve this problem.

Name _____ Date _____

Name Their Ages

Joe's age is twice Rita's age. Ellen is 3 years younger than Rita. The sum of their ages is 13. How old is each child?

Explain the strategy you used to solve this problem.

Use Logical Reasoning
Practice Problems

Logical Reasoning Manipulatives
Circle, triangle, square, rectangle

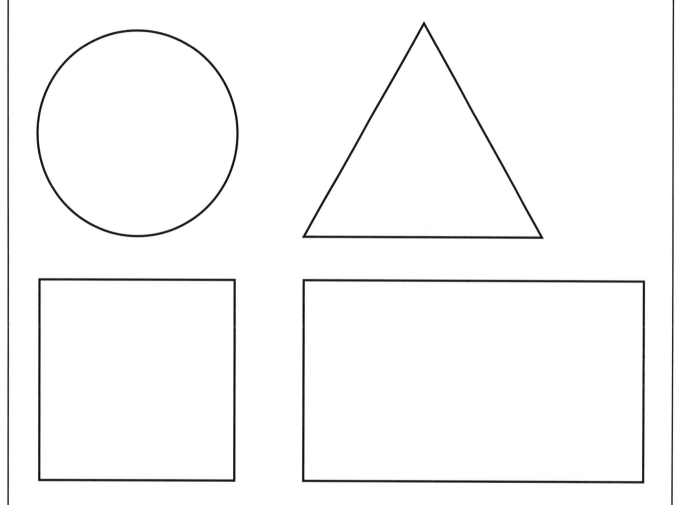

Name _____ Date _____

How Old Is Kim?

How old is Kim?

Use the clues to help you figure out her age.

1. She is less than 10 years old.
2. She is more than 7 years old.
3. She is not 8 years old.

How old is Kim? ___

How do you know?

Name _____ Date _____

Ice Cream Scoops

Your ice cream cone has four scoops of ice cream. Each scoop is a different flavor—chocolate, strawberry, lemon, and vanilla. Read the clues below to help you find out the order of the scoops.

1. The scoop of lemon will be the last one you will eat.
2. The chocolate is right above the lemon.
3. The strawberry is not next to the chocolate.

Explain how you solved the problem.

Name _____ Date _____

Snowy Day Fun

Kelly, Ben, and Rosemary were playing in the snow. One was making snow angels, one was building a snowman, and one was sledding. Kelly did not want to make snow angels. Ben needed a carrot and some buttons. Which person was doing each snow activity?

	snow angels	snowman	sledding
Kelly			
Ben			
Rosemary			

Explain how you solved the problem.

Name _____ Date _____

After-School Snacks

Ryan, Katie, Steven, and Andrew had snacks after school. The snacks were a banana, yogurt, peanuts, and a chocolate bar. Use the clues below to help you figure out which child ate which snack.

▌ Ryan had to peel his snack.
▌ Katie does not like chocolate.
▌ Steven needed a spoon for his snack.

	banana	yogurt	peanuts	chocolate bar
Ryan				
Katie				
Steven				
Andrew				

How did using a matrix help you solve the problem?

Name _____ Date _____

Colorful Flowers

Rita got three flowers on Valentine's Day. She got a rose, a daisy, and a carnation. One flower was red, one was yellow, and one was white. The daisy was not yellow. The carnation matched the color of her new red vase. What color was each flower?

Explain how you solved the problem.

Name _____ Date _____

Team Treats

The coach brought the ten players on Brendan's basketball team to the ice cream parlor to celebrate their big win. The players could order an ice cream cone, a soft drink, or both. Seven players had ice cream and six players had a soft drink. How many players had both?

Explain the strategy you used to solve this problem.

Name _____ Date _____

Cookies and Cocoa

After playing in the snow, 12 children went inside for a snack. 8 children had hot cocoa and 9 children had cookies. How many children had both?

Explain how you solved the problem.

Name _____ Date _____

The Library Schedule

At Glenn Dale Elementary School, Mrs. McConn, Mrs. Little, Mrs. Mack, Mr. Flin, and Miss Black all bring their classes to the school library on a different day of the week. Use the clues below to figure out which day each class goes to the library.

1. Either Miss Black's class or Mrs. McConn's class goes to the library on Wednesdays. The other class goes on Thursdays.
2. Mr. Flin's class goes to the library on a day whose name begins with the letter "T."
3. Mrs. Mack's class goes to the library two days before Miss Black's class.

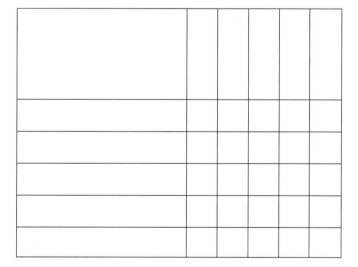

Explain how you were able to figure out which day Mrs. Little's class goes to the library.

Name _____ Date _____

How Many Students?

Use the clues to figure out how many students are in Amanda's class.

- It is less than 35.
- It is a multiple of 4.
- It is more than 25.
- The two digits add up to 5.

Explain how you solved this problem.

Work Backward
Practice Problems

Work Backward Manipulative
Pattern—bag for candy

candy

Name _____ Date _____

The Piggy Bank

Kara bought a book for 50¢. She has 21¢ left in her piggy bank. How much did she have to start?

Explain how you solved the problem.

Name _____ Date _____

Burger Barn

Mrs. Higgins went to Burger Barn. She spent half of the money she had on lunch. Then, she spent 75¢ on dessert. She had $1.00 left. How much money did she have at the start?

Explain how you solved the problem.

Name _____ Date _____

The Trip to School

Ernie got to school at 8:20 a.m. It took him 15 minutes to walk to the bus stop. He spent 10 minutes waiting for the bus. The bus ride took 11 minutes. What time did he leave his house in the morning?

Explain the strategy you used to solve the problem.

Name _____ Date _____

Going Bowling

Pat went bowling. First, he spent half of his money to rent bowling shoes and pay for the games he bowled. Then, he spent $2.75 at the snack bar. He had $3.15 left. How much money did Pat have at the start?

Why is working backward a good strategy for solving this problem?

Name _____ Date _____

The Hike

A group of campers decided to go on a hike around the lake. Half of the campers decided they were too tired and turned around. Five campers decided to go for a swim in the lake instead of finishing the hike. Seven campers got a ride back to camp in the park ranger's van. Nine campers were left to finish the hike around the lake. How many campers were there when they started the hike?

Explain the strategy you used to solve the problem.

Name _____ Date _____

Baseball Cards

David bought some baseball cards. He gave half of the cards he bought to Tyvone. Then he gave half of what he had left to Sherri. After that he had 12 cards. How many cards did he buy?

Explain how you solved the problem.

Name _____ Date _____

The Big Snow

Mrs. Pinson went to the grocery store to get ready for the big snow. First, she spent half of her money on food. Then, she spent $6.30 on some logs for the fire. On the way home, she spent another $15.00 to fill her car with gas. When she got home, she had $20.00 left. How much did Mrs. Pinson have at the start?

Which strategy did you choose to solve this problem? Why?

Appendix H
Real-World
Problem-Solving Resources

Sports Stat Math

Following are some examples of questions that can be answered using the sports box scores that appear in the local newspaper. Teachers might want to use a few as a warm-up activity or place them at a classroom center for individual student use. Students will need to apply their math problem-solving skills, as well as their computation skills, to answer the questions related to the game. Teachers should select questions that match students' skill level.

Basketball

- Which player(s) scored the most points? Least?
- Which player(s) had the most rebounds?
- Which player played the longest (minutes)?
- Which player had the best free-throw percentage for the game?
- What was the average number of points scored by players on each team?
- What was the score after the first quarter? Second quarter? Third quarter?
- Select two players from yesterday's game. Make a table to compare their game stats. Which player had a better game? Justify your answer.

Baseball

- How many more runs would the losing team have had to score to win the game?
- How many runs did the two teams score together?
- Which player(s) had the best batting average for yesterday's game?
- Order the players from best to worst batting for yesterday's game.
- Who would you choose as Most Valuable Player in yesterday's game? Use data to justify your answer.

Football

- By how many points did your team win or lose?
- How long was the longest field goal completed? The shortest? What was the difference between the two?
- Which quarterback had the best completion percentage?

Hockey

- What was the score after the first period? The second?
- Which team had the most shots on goal?
- What was the average number of shots on goal for each period?
- Which goalie had the most saves? Which goalie had the best saves percentage?

Travel Brochure Math

A variety of travel brochures can be found that provide data for performance tasks similar to the following.

For Brochures That List Admission Costs Based on Age or Adult/Child Rates

Calculating the Cost of a Class Field Trip

Part I   Your class has decided to go on a field trip to (name of attraction). Your teacher has asked you to determine how much the trip will cost. (name of attraction) requires one adult chaperone for every ten students (round off the number of students to the nearest ten). Your teacher counts as an adult chaperone. Indicate the number of students and adult chaperones below.

     _____students
     _____adult chaperones

Use the information on the brochure to determine the total cost of admission to (name of attraction).

     cost for students = _____
     cost for adults = _____
     total cost = _____

Explain how you got your answer.

Part II   The cost of the bus is $_____. What is the total cost for both the bus and admission to (name of attraction)?

Your teacher does not want chaperones to have to pay for the trip, so the cost of admission and bus will have to be divided among the students. How much will each student have to pay for the trip? _____

Explain how you decided on the price to charge each student.

For Brochures That Give Individual Admission Rates and a Family Rate

Finding the Best Admission Rate

List the names and ages of the members of your family.

(Name of attraction) charges admission for individuals or for a whole family. If your family were to visit, would it be cheaper to pay for each person separately or to pay the family rate?

_____

Use data from the brochure to justify your answer.

For Brochures That List a Series of Events and the Times That Each Event Occurs

Planning Your Day

Your class will be taking a field trip to (name of attraction). You must stay with a partner, so your teacher has asked you to work with your partner to plan your day. Use the information on the brochure to help you decide what you and your partner will do during your visit.

You will be leaving school at (time). The bus ride takes 20 minutes.

You must schedule lunch (at least 30 minutes) and some time to shop for souvenirs (at least 20 minutes).

Your teacher told everyone to see (list one or two events from the brochure).

You will need to be back at school by (time).

List your schedule for the day below, including the time and name of each event.

For Brochures That Include a Map and Map Scale or for City or State Maps

Planning a Trip

Part I   Your group is planning a trip to (<u>name of city or state</u>). Using the map, decide on three places that you would like to visit. Using the map scale and a ruler or piece of string, determine the approximate mileage you will travel during your trip to visit these locations. You will begin and end your trip at the same location (whichever you choose).

Location #1_____
Location #2_____
Location #3_____

Miles traveled from location #1 to #2_____
Miles traveled from location #2 to #3_____
Miles traveled from location #3 to #1_____
Total trip mileage_____

Explain how you were able to determine the number of miles between each location.

Part II   You have decided on the three locations you will be visiting. Your chaperones prefer not to drive more than (*specify a number*) miles each day. How many days will your trip take? Plan where (in which city) you will stop each night. Explain your plans for your trip.

Part III   Your group will need to give the driver directions for the trip. Use map directions to explain the routes you will take. (*for example, We will begin in Tampa and travel southeast on Route 75 to Fort Lauderdale . . . .*)

State Tourist Board Offices

Students can request information from state tourism offices. Many states send free travel brochures, road maps, and other tourist information that is filled with data that can be used for classroom travel activities.

Note: All World Wide Web addresses begin with *http://*.

Alabama Bureau of Tourism and Travel
800/252-2262
www.touralabama.org

Alaska Division of Tourism
907/465-2012
www.dced.state.ak.us/tourism/

Arizona Office of Tourism
800/842-8257
www.arizonaguide.com

Arkansas Department of Parks and Tourism
800/NATURAL (800/628-8725)
www.1800natural.com

California Division of Tourism
800/862-2543
www.gocalif.ca.gov

Colorado Travel and Tourism Authority
800/265-6723
www.colorado.com

Connecticut Department of Economic Development, Tourism Division
800/CTBOUND (800/282-6863)
www.tourism.state.ct.us

Delaware Tourism Office
800/441-8846
www.state.de.us

Washington D.C. Convention and Visitors Association
202/789-7000
www.washington.org

Florida Division of Tourism
888/735-2872
www.flausa.com

Georgia Department of Industry/Trade/Tourism
800/847-4842
www.georgia.org/itt/tourism/

Hawaii Visitors Bureau
808/923-1811
www.gohawaii.com

Idaho Division of Travel Promotion
800/635-7820
www.visitid.org

Illinois Bureau of Tourism
800/223-0121
www.enjoyillinois.com

Indiana Tourism
800/759-9191
www.state.in.us/tourism

Iowa Division of Tourism
800/345-4692
www.traveliowa.com

Kansas Division of Travel & Tourism
800/252-6727
www.kansascommerce.com

Kentucky Department of Travel Development
800/225-8747
www.state.ky.us/tour/tour.htm

Louisiana Office of Tourism
800/334-8626
www.louisianatravel.com

Maine Publicity Bureau
800/533-9595
www.visitmaine.com

Maryland Office of Tourism Development
800/543-1036
www.mdisfun.org

Massachusetts Office of Travel & Tourism
800/447-6277
www.mass-vacation.com

Michigan Department of Commerce, Travel Bureau
800/543-2937
www.michigan.org

Minnesota Office of Tourism
800/657-3700
www.exploreminnesota.com

Mississippi Department of Tourism
800/927-6378
www.visitmississippi.org

Missouri Division of Tourism
800/877-1234
www.missouritourism.org/

Montana Travel
800/541-1447
www.visitmt.com/

Nebraska Tourism Office
800/228-4307
www.visitnebraska.org

Nevada Commission on Tourism
800/638-2328
www.travelnevada.com

New Hampshire Office of Travel and Tourism
800/386-4664
www.visitnh.gov

New Jersey Division of Travel & Tourism
800/537-7397
www.state.nj.us/travel

New Mexico Department of Tourism
800/545-2040
www.newmexico.org

New York State Division of Tourism
800/225-5697
www.iloveny.state.ny.us

North Carolina Division of Travel & Tourism
800/847-4862
www.visitnc.com

North Dakota Department of Tourism
800/437-2077
www.ndtourism.com

Ohio Tourism
800/282-5393
www.ohiotourism.com

Oklahoma Tourism & Recreation Department
800/652-6552
www.otrd.state.ok.us

Oregon Tourism Commission
800/547-7842
www.traveloregon.com

Pennsylvania Tourism
800/847-4872
www.state.pa.us/visit

Rhode Island Tourism Division
800/556-2484
www.visitrhodeisland.com

South Carolina Department of Parks, Recreation & Tourism
800/346-3634
www.sccsi.com/sc

South Dakota Department of Tourism
800/732-5682
www.state.sd.us/tourism/

Tennessee Department of Tourism
800/836-6200
www.state.tn.us/tourdev/

Texas Department of Commerce, Tourism Division
800/888-8839
www.traveltex.com

Utah Travel Council
800/200-1160
www.utah.com

Vermont Department of Travel and Tourism
800/837-6668
www.travel-vermont.com

Virginia Division of Tourism
800/847-4882
www.virginia.org

Washington State Tourism
800/544-1800
www.tourism.wa.gov

West Virginia Tourism
800/225-5982
www.state.wv.us/tourism

Wisconsin Tourism
800/432-8747
www.tourism.state.wi.us

Wyoming Division of Tourism
800/225-5996
www.state.wy.us/state/tourism/tourism.html/

APPENDIX H

Menu Math

The use of a local restaurant menu, like the Antonio's Restaurant menu in Figure H–1, will reinforce students' problem-solving skills. Questions similar to those below require students to apply classroom skills to typical dining situations. While some of the problems can be answered by choosing the correct operation, some of the problems require students to use other problem-solving strategies. A menu and a question of the day might be used as a center activity, or students might solve selected problems individually or with partners during class time.

1. You want to order a 16″ pizza with a lot of toppings. You have $15.00. How many toppings will you be able to buy? How did you figure out your answer?

2. You are having lunch with some friends. You have to decide on toppings for your pizza. Everyone likes pepperoni, sausage, green pepper, and ham. How many different pizza combinations can you make using at least one of these four items? Explain your answer.

3. You order a 10″ × 14″ pizza. The cook cuts it into 2″ × 2″ squares. How many pieces will there be? Explain the strategy you used to figure out the answer.

4. Which is a better buy—a 12″ round pizza or a 10″ × 14″ pizza? Justify your answer.

5. You have $10.00 to spend for lunch. Decide what you would like to have. Write the name of each item you will order. What will the total cost of your lunch be? How much change will you receive? Explain how you got your answer.

6. Your family has asked you to order the family dinner at Antonio's. Order a meal for each member of your family. Use a calculator to help you determine the cost. (Be sure to add tax or a delivery charge.)

7. What is the least expensive meal (dinner and drink) that you can find on the menu? The most expensive? Justify your answer.

8. You would like a salad and a drink. You can choose a garden salad, tuna salad, or chef salad. You can choose a Coke, Sprite, or fruit punch. How many salad/drink combinations are possible? Make a list to justify your answer.

9. Drinks are sold in 12 oz., 16 oz., and 20 oz. sizes. Which size drink is a better buy? Justify your answer.

10. If you order a garden salad and a piece of cheesecake, can you have it delivered? Why or why not?

11. Katie ordered a kid's meal and a drink. Together it cost $4.40. Which kid's meal and which size drink did she order?

12. Brendan spent $3.10 on a sub and a drink. Then he spent half of what he had left on dessert. Finally, he spent $.80 on a tip. When he left Antonio's he had $1.70. How much did he have when he went into the restaurant? Explain the strategy you used to find the answer.

182

Antonio's

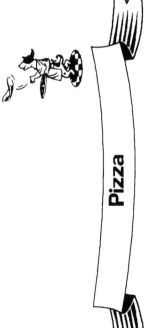

Pizza

	10" round	12" round	16" round	10" x 14"
plain	$4.50	$6.50	$9.25	$6.50
per item	$.75	$1.10	$1.25	$1.10

Toppings: Pepperoni, sausage, mushrooms, black olives, ham, green pepper, onion, bacon, extra cheese

Subs

	4"	8"
	$2.50	$4.19
extra cheese	$.15	$.30

Steak and Cheese, Meatball and Cheese, Ham and Cheese, Turkey and Cheese, Italian, Tuna Fish, Veggie

Kid's Menu

All dinners include a roll and salad.

Spaghetti.............$3.50
Cheese Ravioli.......$4.85

Dinners

All dinners include a rolll and tossed salad

Spaghetti with Tomato Sauce.......$5.25
Spaghetti with Meatsauce...........$6.25
Spaghetti with Meatballs............$6.25
Meat Lasagna........................$7.25
Cheese Ravioli......................$7.25

Salads

Garden salad $2.50
Tuna Salad $3.99
Chef Salad $3.99

Italian, Lo Cal Italian, 1000 Island, Ranch, French dressings

Drinks

12 oz.	16 oz.	20 oz.
$.60	$.75	$.90

Pitchers $2.25
Coffee $.90

Desserts

Cheesecake $1.95
Ice Cream Sundae $2.50
Brownie $1.00

Minimum Delivery - $6.00
Prices do not include tax. There is a
$.75 delivery charge.

FIGURE H–1

Recipe Books

Following are examples of recipe books that contain recipes with kid appeal. The recipe data can be used to create a variety of problem-solving activities.

Demauro, L. 1987. *Chocolate Heaven*. New York: Parachute.

Ellison, S., and J. Gray. 1995. *365 Foods Kids Love to Eat*. Naperville, IL: Sourcebooks.

Gillis, J. S. 1992. *In a Pumpkin Shell*. New York: Scholastic.

Gordon, L. 1996. *Messipes*. New York: Random House.

Great-Tasting Kids' Snacks. 1995. Lincolnwood, IL: Publications International.

JELL-O Kids' Cooking Fun. 1991. Glenview, IL: Kraft General Foods.

Kuntz, L., and J. Fleming. 1997. *American Grub*. New York: Scholastic.

Linton, M. 1986. *Just Desserts*. Buffalo, NY: Kids Can.

Marx, P. 1996. *Travel the World Cookbook*. Glenview, IL: GoodYear.

Moore, E. 1973. *The Cookie Book*. New York: Scholastic.

Poppin' Fresh Homemade Cookies. 1993. Baltimore: Ottenheimer.

Robins, D. 1994. *The Kids' Around the World Cookbook*. New York: Kingfisher.

Williamson, S., and Z. Williamson. 1992. *Kids Cook!* Charlotte, VT: Williamson.

Admission Data for Student Problems

Data similar to the following will serve to motivate students and show them the connection between classroom skills and real-world applications. Teachers might ask students to write their own problems using this data or teachers might create problems for students to solve. In each sample, special deals, such as consecutive-day savings, sunset savings, annual passes, and family rates, create problem-solving opportunities that require students to combine their reasoning skills with their computational skills. Real data from local attractions will provide motivation and true data for your students to consider.

Sample Amusement Park Admissions

Regular (ages 9–54)..$29.95
Junior (ages 3–8)..$16.95
Senior (ages 55+)..$16.95
Children (ages 2 and younger) ....free
Consecutive Day...$18.95
Sunset Savings (ages 3 & older) $15.95
    (admission after 5pm)

Sample questions

▌ If your family went to the park for two days, how much would you save if you bought Consecutive Day passes? Explain.
▌ Are Consecutive Day passes a good deal for everyone in your family? Explain.
▌ Are there any other deals that might save your family money? Explain.

Sample Zoo Admissions

Adults..$6.75
Children 3–12 ....$4.00
Children under 3...free
Unlimited Annual Family Visits $50.00

Sample question

▌ How many times would your family have to visit the zoo to make the Unlimited Annual Visits ticket a better buy? Justify your answer using math data.

Sample Museum Admissions

Adults..$5.00
Children 4–16 ....$3.00
Children under 4...free
Family rate..$15.00

Sample question

▌ Which is a better deal for your family—buying individual admission tickets or entering under the family rate? Justify your answer using math data.

Appendix I
Parent Letter-Tips for Helping Your Child Get "Unstuck"

Dear Parent,

Does your child ever get "stuck" when solving math problems? Does he or she get frustrated and want to quit? One important lesson in problem solving is to keep trying, even if an answer is not found after the first few tries. You can help your child develop strategies to get "unstuck." Following are some ideas that might help:

Jot Down Ideas

Jot down a plan for how you will be solving the problem. You might list the important information or draw a diagram of the problem to get you started.

Restate the Problem in Your Own Words

Are you unsure how to begin? Reread the problem and then state it in your own words. You need to understand the problem before you can go any further.

Cross Off Unnecessary Information

Is the problem confusing, containing too much data? Reread the problem and cross out the unnecessary data to simplify the problem.

Substitute with Simpler Numbers

Does the problem contain large numbers or fractions or decimals that are confusing you? Substitute simpler numbers for the confusing numbers and then figure out how to solve the problem. Once you know how the problem should be solved, just plug the more complicated numbers back into the problem and repeat the process to solve it.

Take a Break

Are you too frustrated to go on? Take a break for a few minutes. Think about or do something else. Then return to the problem refreshed and ready to begin again.

Use a Manipulative

Use everyday objects (paper clips, toothpicks, pennies) to represent the items in the problem. Act out the problem with the manipulatives.

Talk the Problem Through

Talk out loud to yourself or to someone else. Explain the problem and what you think you should do. Listen to yourself as you talk to see if it makes sense.

Think of a Similar Problem

Does this problem remind you of another that you've solved? How did you solve that one? Try that strategy. Does it work here?

Try a Different Strategy

What you're doing doesn't seem to be working. Try something else. Is there a different strategy that you think might work? Try it and see.

Give Yourself a Pep Talk

Think of a problem you solved by sticking with it. Remember a time when you were frustrated but kept on trying until you found the answer. Remind yourself that you can do it!

Model these ideas for your child. Show him or her how to keep calm, think a problem through, and try again. Your encouragement of their efforts and your suggestions for ways to get themselves "unstuck" will help them grow into successful problem solvers. Thanks for your help!

Sincerely,

References

Bloomer, A. M., R. I. Charles, and F. K. Lester Jr. 1996. *Problem Solving Experiences in Mathematics (Grade K)*. Menlo Park, CA: Addison-Wesley.

Brinker, L. 1998. "Using Recipes and Ratio Tables." *Teaching Children Mathematics* 5 (4): 218–24.

Burns, M. 1982. *Math for Smarty Pants*. Boston: Little, Brown & Co.

———. 1987. *A Collection of Math Lessons from Grades 3 Through 6*. New York: Math Solutions.

———. 1992. *About Teaching Mathematics*. New York: Math Solutions.

Campbell, P. 1997. "Connecting Instructional Practice to Student Thinking." *Teaching Children Mathematics* 4 (2): 106–10.

Charles, R. I. and F. K. Lester Jr. 1985. *Problem Solving Experiences in Mathematics (Grade 3)*. Menlo Park, CA: Addison-Wesley.

Charles, R. I., F. K. Lester Jr., and A. Bloomer. 1996a. *Problem Solving Experiences in Mathematics (Grade 1)*. Menlo Park, CA: Addison-Wesley.

———. 1996b. *Problem Solving Experiences in Mathematics (Grade 2)*. Menlo Park, CA: Addison-Wesley.

Charles, R. I., R. P. Mason, and G. Gallagher. 1985. *Problem Solving Experiences in Mathematics (Grade 5)*. Menlo Park, CA: Addison-Wesley.

Charles, R. I., R. P. Mason, and D. Garner. 1985. *Problem Solving Experiences in Mathematics (Grade 6)*. Menlo Park, CA: Addison-Wesley.

Charles, R. I., R. P. Mason, and L. Martin. 1985. *Problem Solving Experiences in Mathematics (Grade 4)*. Menlo Park, CA: Addison-Wesley.

Charles, R. I., and E. A. Silver, eds. 1989. *The Teaching and Assessing of Mathematical Problem Solving*. Reston, VA: National Council of Teachers of Mathematics.

Coburn, T. G. 1993. *NCTM Addenda Series—Patterns*. Reston, VA: National Council of Teachers of Mathematics.

Economopoulis, K. 1998. "What Comes Next? The Mathematics of Pattern in Kindergarten." *Teaching Children Mathematics* 5 (4): 230–33.

English, L. 1992. "Problem Solving with Combinations." *Arithmetic Teacher* 40 (2): 72–77.

Ferrini-Mundy, J., G. Lappan, and E. Phillips. 1997. "Experiences with Patterning." *Teaching Children Mathematics* 3 (6): 282–88.

Forsten, C. 1992. *Teaching Thinking and Problem Solving in Math*. New York: Scholastic.

Giglio Andrews, A. 1997. "Doing What Comes Naturally: Talking about Mathematics." *Teaching Children Mathematics* 3 (5): 236–39.

Hogeboom, S., and J. Goodnow. 1987. *The Problem Solver I Series*. Mountain View, CA: Creative.

Johnson, D. R. 1994. *Motivation Counts—Teaching Techniques That Work*. Palo Alto, CA: Dale Seymour.

Kelly, J. A. 1999. "Improving Problem Solving through Drawings." *Teaching Children Mathematics* 6(1): 48–51.

Kroll, D. L. , J. O. Masingila, and S. T. Mau. 1992. "Cooperative Problem Solving: But What about Grading?" *Arithmetic Teacher* 39 (6): 17–23.

Krulik, S., and J. A. Rudnick. 1994. "Reflect . . . For Better Problem Solving and Reasoning." *Arithmetic Teacher* 41 (6): 334–38.

Meyer, C., and T. Sallee. 1983. *Make It Simpler: A Practical Guide to Problem Solving in Mathematics*. Menlo Park, CA: Addison-Wesley.

National Council of Teachers of Mathematics. 1989. *Curriculum and Evaluation Standards for School Mathematics*. Reston, VA: National Council of Teachers of Mathematics.

———. 1991. *Professional Standards for Teaching Mathematics*. Reston, VA: National Council of Teachers of Mathematics.

———. 1995. *Assessment Standards for School Mathematics*. Reston, VA: National Council of Teachers of Mathematics.

O'Connell, S. R. 1992. "Math Pairs—Parents as Partners." *Arithmetic Teacher* 40 (1): 10–12.

———. 1995. "Newspapers: Connecting the Mathematics Classroom to the World." *Teaching Children Mathematics* 1 (5): 268–74.

———. 1998a. *Real World Math for Grades 1–3*. Torrance, CA: Good Apple.

———. 1998b. *Real World Math for Grades 4–6*. Torrance, CA: Good Apple.

———. 2001. *Math—The Write Way*. 3 vols. Torrance, CA: Good Apple.

O'Daffer, P. G., ed. 1988. *Problem Solving Tips for Teachers*. Reston, VA: National Council of Teachers of Mathematics.

Post, B., and S. Eads. 1996. *Logic, Anyone?* Torrance, CA: Fearon Teacher Aids.

Reeves, C. A. 1987. *Problem-Solving Techniques Helpful in Mathematics and Science*. Reston, VA: National Council of Teachers of Mathematics.

Schoenfield, M. and J. Rosenblatt. 1985a. *Discovering Logic*. Belmont, CA: David S. Lake.

———. 1985b. *Playing with Logic*. Belmont, CA: David S. Lake.

Shaw, J. M., M. S. Chambless, D. A. Chessin, V. Price, and G. Beardain. 1997. "Cooperative Problem Solving: Using K–W–D–L as an Organizational Technique." *Teaching Children Mathematics* 3 (9): 482–86.

Smith, K. 1996. *Math Logic Puzzles*. New York: Sterling.

Stenmark, J. K., ed. 1991. *Mathematics Assessment—Myths, Models, Good Questions, and Practical Suggestions*. Reston, VA: National Council of Teachers of Mathematics.

Zawojewski, J. S. 1991. *NCTM Addenda Series—Dealing with Data and Chance*. Reston, VA: National Council of Teachers of Mathematics.